EXPRESS REVIEW GUIDES

Spelling

P9-DGD-229

12.95

AE
428.1
S743 l

EXPRESS REVIEW GUIDES

Spelling

LEARNINGEXPRESS ®

New York

Copyright © 2008 LearningExpress, LLC.

All rights reserved under International and Pan-American Copyright Conventions. Published in the United States by LearningExpress, LLC, New York.

Library of Congress Cataloging-in-Publication Data:

Express review guides. Spelling.
    p. cm.
ISBN: 978-1-57685-651-2 (pbk. : alk. paper)
1. English language—Orthography and spelling—Problems,
exercises, etc. I. LearningExpress (Organization) II. Title: Spelling.
  PE1143.E97 2008
  428.1'3—dc22

                         008019360

Printed in the United States of America

9 8 7 6 5 4 3 2 1

First Edition

ISBN: 978-1-57685-651-2

For more information or to place an order, contact LearningExpress at:
    2 Rector Street
    26th Floor
    New York, NY 10006

Or visit us at:
    www.learnatest.com

Contents

ABOUT THE CONTRIBUTOR vii

INTRODUCTION ix

PRETEST 1

CHAPTER 1 Rule the Rules—*Smart Strategies for Star Spellers* 13

CHAPTER 2 Which Word Is Which? *Homonyms and Commonly Confused Words* 29

CHAPTER 3 Building Words 53

CHAPTER 4 Vowels—*The Long and the Short of It All* 71

CHAPTER 5 The Consistent Consonant 91

CHAPTER 6 This Is How It Ends—*Suffixes* 109

CHAPTER 7 I'll Take Two—*Plurals* 125

CHAPTER 8 Feeling Tense? *Verb Conjugation* 145

CHAPTER 9 201 Commonly Misspelled Words 171

CHAPTER 10 The Living Language 191

POSTTEST 215

APPENDIX A *Master Word List* 227

APPENDIX B *Glossary of English Terms and Difficult Words* 249

APPENDIX C *Pronunciation Guide* 259

APPENDIX D *Prefixes, Suffixes, and Word Roots* 263

About the Contributor

Jeffrey Dinsmore is a writer based in Los Angeles. He has written and edited educational materials for school systems around the country, including LearningExpress's *411 SAT Critical Reading Questions* and *Express Review Guides: Vocabulary*. In addition, he has written two fictional novels—*Johnny Astronaut* (under the pseudonym Rory Carmichael) and *I, An Actress: The Autobiography of Karen Jamey*—both published by Contemporary Press.

Introduction

On June 15, 1992, Vice President Dan Quayle was visiting an elementary school in Trenton, NJ, when a teacher at the school asked him to help with a spelling bee. Vice President Quayle was put in charge of reading the words to the students who were participating in the bee. The vice president would read a word out loud, and then each student would have to write his or her word on the blackboard. Students who spelled their words correctly got to move on to the next round.

The vice president read a few words to students as reporters from newspapers around the country looked on. Finally, it came time for a sixth-grader named William Figueroa to take his turn. Vice President Quayle read William's word: *potato*. William walked up to the board and spelled the word correctly.

Vice President Quayle looked at the word and quietly said to William, "You're close, but you left a little something off. The *e* on the end." William was pretty sure he had spelled the word correctly, but he didn't want to disagree with the vice president. He added an *e*, so the word was spelled *potatoe*, then sat back down in his seat.

The story of the vice president's mistake quickly became national news. Everywhere in the country, people were talking about it. In fact, years later, political cartoonists and late-night talk shows are *still* making jokes about the vice president's spelling mistake. As Quayle wrote in his autobiography, "It was a defining moment of the worst kind imaginable."

Today, many people do not know that Dan Quayle was a successful lawyer and newspaper publisher. They don't know that he was the youngest person from Indiana ever elected to the U.S. Senate, or that he was a well-liked senator who was reelected by a huge margin. But to this day, if you ask almost any adult in America about Dan Quayle, one of the first things they will remember about him is that he didn't know how to spell the word *potato*.

The reaction to Vice President Quayle's mistake shows something very important about spelling: "Close enough" doesn't count. One can understand why the vice president made his mistake; after all, the plural of *potato* is spelled *potatoes*. All he did was add one tiny *e* where it didn't belong. Still, that tiny *e* was enough to make worldwide news and to assure that Vice President Quayle would spend the rest of his life talking about that moment in the classroom.

When the vice president made his mistake, most of the cartoons and jokes painted him as someone who was not very bright. For people in positions of high power, correct spelling is considered a sign of intelligence.

In reality, spelling ability has a lot more to do with practice than intelligence. Many very intelligent people have trouble with spelling. There are an awful lot of rules to remember in spelling, and even when you know all the rules, there are still exceptions. For example, as we learned in the last paragraph, the plural of *potato* is *potatoes*. Likewise, the plural of *tomato* is *tomatoes*, the plural of *echo* is *echoes*, and the plural of *hero* is *heroes*. The pattern here is obvious: If a word ends in *-o*, then you have to add *-es* to make the plural, right? Not so fast. The plural of *piano* isn't *pianoes*; it's *pianos*. The plural of *video* is *videos*, the plural of *radio* is *radios*, and the plural of *studio* is *studios*. In some cases, there are multiple ways you can write the plural; for instance, the plural of *tornado* can be spelled *tornados* or *tornadoes*. Sometimes the plurals don't seem to make any sense; for example, the plural of the word *solo* can be written either as *solos* or *soli*!

Words like *soli* and *tornadoes* are exceptions. The more you know about words, the easier spelling will become. Although there are always words that don't fit some of the rules, the majority of words follow common, easy-to-learn patterns. As you read the chapters and do the practice problems in this book, you will become familiar with many of these typical spelling patterns. Once you learn these patterns, your spelling will improve. And in 40 years, when you are the vice president, you can be sure no one will remember you as the person who didn't know how to spell *potato*!

CAUTION!

THE RISE OF the personal computer has brought with it a powerful new tool with which you are no doubt familiar: the spell check. Bad spellers everywhere rejoiced when spell check first became available. No longer did they have to comb through dictionaries and tediously check each word in their letters and documents; spell check did the work for them. Now, thanks to spell check, we are finally living in a glorious new era in which spelling errors are a thing of the past.

Of course, you know this isn't entirely true. Spell check is very good at fixing careless mistakes, but it's lousy at guessing what someone is trying to say. If you accidentally type the word *teh* instead of *the*, chances are good that spell check will catch your mistake. But, if you use the word *site* where you mean to use the word *sight*, or *sight* where you mean to use *might*, spell check will skip right over it.

In addition, spell check usually only recognizes the most common misspellings of words. It will alert you if you've spelled a word it doesn't recognize, but unless your error is extremely common, your computer may not have any idea what word you meant to use. And all you can do in that case is flip open a dictionary, just like in the old days.

Until we develop technology smart enough to understand exactly what we're trying to say at all times, it is still very important that we learn how to spell. And technology aside, spelling is definitely a skill worth honing. Good spelling and grammar skills lead to good communications skills, and those who communicate well have a greater chance of succeeding in life. Take the time to learn the words in this book and you'll be on the right path!

HOW TO USE THIS BOOK

Immediately following this section, you will find a pretest that measures your current spelling abilities. The pretest can help you see the areas in which you could use some help. Don't worry if you don't do very well on the pretest; you may have never learned some of the skills taught in this book before. By the end of the book, you should be able to recognize all of the words in the pretest and understand why they are spelled the way they are.

Following the pretest are ten skill-building chapters. Each chapter discusses one skill that will be important to improving your spelling. Although you may use this book any way you choose, the best way to build your skills is to go through the chapters in order. Here is a brief outline of each chapter:

Chapter 1: Rule the Rules—Smart Strategies for Star Spellers teaches some helpful tricks for studying spelling.

Chapter 2: Which Word Is Which? Homonyms and Commonly Confused Words talks about words that are often confused because they sound alike or have similar meanings.

Chapter 3: Building Words discusses the basic building blocks of words—roots, prefixes, and suffixes—and how knowledge of these parts can help make you a better speller.

Chapter 4: Vowels—The Long and the Short of It All talks about the five (sometimes six) vowels and how they fit into words.

Chapter 5: The Consistent Consonant describes the other 21 letters in the alphabet and their many combinations.

Chapter 6: This Is How It Ends—Suffixes teaches you all you need to know about adding suffix endings to words.

Chapter 7: I'll Take Two—Plurals discusses the rules for turning singular nouns into plural nouns.

Chapter 8: Feeling Tense? Conjugating Verbs reviews the many rules and exceptions behind subject-verb agreement.

Chapter 9: 201 Commonly Misspelled Words goes over the 201 most commonly misspelled words in the English language and tips for spelling them correctly.

Chapter 10: The Living Language talks about new words that are coming into the English language and other words that are important to learn.

The *Express Review Guides* series also includes the following features:

➥ *Fuel for Thought*: critical information and definitions that can help you learn more about a particular topic

➡ *Practice Lap*: quick practice exercises and activities to let you test your knowledge

➡ *Inside Track*: tips for reducing your study and practice time—without sacrificing accuracy

➡ *Caution!* Pitfalls to be on the lookout for

After the chapters, a posttest is included that makes use of the different skills and words taught in the book. If you've read the book carefully and completed the practice questions, you'll be amazed at how much you've improved since the pretest!

At the end of the book are four appendices. **Appendix A** lists all of the words that appeared in the end-of-chapter word lists. **Appendix B** defines the more difficult words and terms found in the book. **Appendix C** provides a guide for pronunciation symbols used in the book. **Appendix D** is a list of common roots, prefixes, and suffixes that are useful to know.

Pretest

The following pretest measures your knowledge of spelling fundamentals. Take your time answering the questions. If you don't know an answer, there's no need to guess; this test is designed to measure what you know and not how many answers you can guess correctly. After you're finished, check your answers and see how you've done!

Sentence Completion

This exercise tests your ability to recognize the correct spelling of a word. Each sentence is followed by four answer choices. Choose the answer choice that is spelled correctly and makes the most sense in the sentence.

1. Martin is _____ the first person here in the morning.
   a. usully
   b. usually
   c. useally
   d. useuly

2. Jack will _____ his presents on the morning of his birthday.
   a. resieve
   b. recieve
   c. receive
   d. reseive

3. Make sure to _____ your socks before putting them in the laundry.
   a. separate
   b. seperate
   c. sepurate
   d. seperrate

4. Mr. Fowks has a strong _____ of history.
   a. knowledge
   b. knoledge
   c. knowlege
   d. knollege

5. Please don't _____ me when I'm speaking.
   a. interupt
   b. intterupt
   c. interrupt
   d. innterrupt

6. Julie marked the date on her _____.
   a. calender
   b. calander
   c. calandar
   d. calendar

7. The audience _____ at the end of the performance.
   a. applouds
   b. applauds
   c. applause
   d. appluads

8. It will be difficult to get to the theater on time but _____.
   a. manageable
   b. managable
   c. manageible
   d. managible

9. Open up the _____ program and I'll show you how to make a graph.
   a. spread sheet
   b. spreadshete
   c. spredsheet
   d. spreadsheet

10. Juan is the most _____ friend I have.
    a. loyel
    b. loil
    c. loyal
    d. loial

Choose the Right Spelling

Circle the italicized word that is spelled correctly.

11. It was difficult to (*reconize/recognize*) Sasha after she got her hair cut.

12. I (*posess/possess*) a box of baseball cards that my grandpa gave to me.

13. Angelique's next-door (*neighbor/naybor*) is also her best friend.

14. The phrase *It's always darkest before the dawn* is a well-known (*clishay/cliché*).

15. The old (*semetary/cemetery*) behind the church contains some interesting graves.

16. My dad's boss just gave him an increase in his annual (*salery/salary*).

17. Next year I will be in (*eihth/eighth*) grade.

18. (*February/Febuary*) is Black History Month.

19. It's hard to (*denie/deny*) the influence that George Washington had on our government.

20. The (*nome/gnome*) ran through the forest to get away from the troll.

Homonyms and Commonly Confused Words

The following sentences contain words that are commonly confused. Circle the spelling of the italicized word that best completes the sentence.

21. I love Mexico; we're planning on going (*their/there/they're*) for spring break.

22. In the fall, Terrance will (*attend/intend*) Jefferson Middle School.

23. The car had been stripped (*bare/bear*) of its paint.

24. Ms. Crandell isn't sure (*weather/whether*) or not we will understand *Romeo and Juliet*.

25. Mr. Whitman is the (*principal/principle*) at Victoria Falls High.

26. The warm weather had a positive (*affect/effect*) on Janine's health.

27. Maria tends to (*loose/lose*) her house keys.

28. Take a deep (*breath/breathe*) if you are feeling worried.

29. Amir walks (*passed/past*) the drugstore on his way to school.

30. The blind man had an operation to restore his (*sight/site*).

Suffixes

Combine the following base words with the endings indicated. Write the new word in the blank space.

31. plan + -er = _____

32. joy + -ous = _____

33. know + -able = _____

34. wise + -est = _____

35. horrible + -ly = _____

36. remit + -ance = _____

37. beauty + -ful = _____

38. resist + -ance = _____

39. eager + -ness = _____

40. crazy + -ly = _____

Plurals

Correctly spell the plural forms of the following words.

Singular	Plural
41. moose	_____
42. boundary	_____
43. box	_____
44. knife	_____
45. goose	_____
46. volcano	_____
47. baby	_____
48. self	_____
49. hatch	_____
50. book	_____

Verb Conjugations

Write the present participle, past tense, and past participle of each of the following words. (Note: if you're not sure what these terms mean, turn to the glossary in Appendix B).

Present Tense	Present Participle	Past Tense	Past Participle
51. fall			
52. try			
53. marry			
54. expect			
55. cut			
56. make			
57. compare			
58. lay			
59. break			
60. catch			

ANSWERS

Sentence Completion

1. **b. usually.** (Chapter 9) *Usually* is a word that's filled with difficult spelling and pronunciation gaps. It sounds like it should start with the word *use*, but it does not. It sounds like it should have an *sh*, but it does not. There is an unexpected double-*ll* combination near the end of the word. However, if you can remember how to spell the word *usual*, you

should be able to remember that all you need to do is stick an *-ly* on the end to spell *usually*.

2. **c. receive.** (Chapter 1) Many people confuse the order of *is* and *es* when they are next to each other in a word. One helpful saying to remember is "i before e, except after c." This means that the letter *i* comes before the letter *e* in most words, unless the two words are following the letter *c*, as in *receive*.

3. **a. separate.** (Chapter 4, Chapter 9) When most people pronounce the word *separate*, it sounds like "sep-ur-ayt." When trying to remember how to spell a word, it can be useful to pronounce the word in your mind as it is spelled—"sep-*ar*-ate." *Separate* is a word with an *r*-controlled vowel sound, which you will learn more about in Chapter 4.

4. **a. knowledge.** (Chapter 5) The word *knowledge* is another word that is not pronounced like it is spelled. It can be helpful to create a visual picture for some words. Picture a *ledge* filled with statues of famous philosophers who *know* a lot.

5. **c. interrupt.** (Chapter 5) It can be difficult to remember which consonants are doubled in words with double consonants.

6. **d. calendar.** (Chapter 4) *Calendar* has the schwa sound, which can be difficult to remember. Many people would pick choice **a**, *calender*. This is another example in which it is helpful to memorize the mispronunciation of the word.

7. **b. applauds.** (Chapter 3) To spell *applauds*, it helps to know that the root is *aud*, which means "related to hearing."

8. **a. manageable.** (Chapter 3) Words that can stand on their own like *manage* usually add the suffix *-able* instead of *-ible*.

9. **d. spreadsheet.** (Chapter 3, Chapter 10) *Spreadsheet* is a compound word that is a combination of the words *spread* and *sheet*. It is also a technology word that is useful to learn.

10. **c. loyal.** (Chapter 4) The *oy* sound is known as a diphthong. It is a common vowel + vowel combination that can be found in other words like *joy*, *royal*, and *boy*.

Choose the Right Spelling

11. **recognize.** (Chapter 9) When many people say the word *recognize*, it sounds more like "reck-a-nize." Knowing the proper pronunciation is the key to spelling this word correctly.

12. **possess.** (Chapter 5) *Possess* has two sets of double consonants, which can be difficult to remember.

13. **neighbor.** (Chapter 4) *Neighbor* contains the fairly unusual *eigh* combination, which is pronounced like a long *a*. Fairly unusual but not unheard of—the words *sleigh*, *freight* and *eight* all contain the same combination.

14. **cliché.** (Chapter 10) *Cliché* is a French word meaning "an overused expression."

15. **cemetery.** (Chapter 5) It can be difficult to remember which words have the letter *s* and which words have the letter *c* because they are sometimes pronounced the same way.

16. **salary.** (Chapter 10) *Salary* is a business word that you will need to be able to spell in the future.

17. **eighth.** (Chapter 9) *Eighth* is an unusually spelled number word.

18. **February.** (Chapter 9) *February* is a classically difficult word to spell, due to that awkward *r* stuck in the middle. This is a word that unfortunately just has to be memorized.

19. **deny.** (Chapter 4) The letter *y* can sometimes make the same sound as *ie*, but in this case, the correct spelling is *deny*.

20. **gnome.** (Chapter 5) The letter combination *gn* is known as a digraph. The letter *g* in this word is silent.

Homonyms and Commonly Confused Words

With these words, the problem is not necessarily one of tricky letter combinations. More often than not, the reason these words are misspelled is because one word has been confused for another word that sounds similar. You can find out more information about commonly confused words in Chapter 2.

21. **there.** *They're* is a contraction for *they are*, and *their* means "owned by them"; therefore, the correct answer is *there*, which means "in or at that place."

22. **attend.** *Intend* means "plan to." *Attend* means "to go to." Terrance will "go to" Jefferson Middle School, so *attend* is the best choice.

23. **bare.** *Bear* is an animal, while *bare* is an adjective. The correct answer here is *bare*.

24. **whether.** *Weather* and *whether* are often confused. *Weather* refers to temperature and climate, while *whether* is a conjunction that is used to introduce sets of alternatives. *Whether* is the correct choice in this circumstance.

25. **principal.** This is another extremely common mistake, since *principal* and *principle* only differ in their final two letters. *Principle* means "primary," while a *principal* is the person who runs a school. In this case, a mnemonic device can be a helpful memory tool, like "The princi*pal* is your *pal*." You can read more about mnemonic devices in Chapter 1.

26. **effect.** You can tell from context that this sentence requires a noun. The word *effect* is a noun, meaning "result." The word *affect* is generally used as a verb, meaning "to have an influence on." The correct choice here is *effect*.

27. **lose.** This is a common mistake that can easily be prevented if you take the time to sound the words out. *Loose* has the double-*o* sound like *moo* in the middle, while *lose* has an *s* that sounds like a *z*. *Loose* means "not tight," while *lose* means "unable to find."

28. **breath.** *Breath* is a noun, while *breathe* is a verb. In this case, it helps to know that a noun is the part of speech that belongs here. In this case, the correct choice is *breath*.

29. **past.** Like *loose* and *lose*, this is another common mistake that can be prevented by sounding the words out. If you spoke this sentence out loud, you would say he walked *past* the drugstore, with a hard *t* sound. *Passed* is the past tense of *pass*, while *past* means "beyond." The correct choice here is *past*.

30. **sight.** *Sight* refers to vision, while a *site* is a place, like a construction site. The correct answer for this sentence is *sight*.

Suffixes

The rules for combining suffixes with base words are pretty consistent. You can read about these rules in Chapter 6.

31. **planner.** When adding a word that ends in a consonant + vowel + consonant combination to a suffix that begins with a vowel, double the final consonant.

32. **joyous.** Words that end in vowel + -*y* combinations do not change when adding suffixes.

33. **knowable.** Most words that end in consonant + vowel + consonant combinations double the final consonant when adding suffixes that begin with vowels; the exception are words that end in -*w* or -*x*.

34. **wisest.** Drop the silent *e* when adding suffixes that begin with vowel to base words that end in a silent *e*.

35. **horribly.** When a base word ends in -*ible*, replace the final *e* with a -*y* to make it into an adverb.

36. **remittance.** When a base word of more than one syllable ends in the consonant + vowel + consonant combination *and* the accent is on the final syllable, double the final consonant when adding a suffix that begins with a vowel.

37. **beautiful.** Words that end in consonant + -*y* combinations change the final *y* to an *i* when adding suffixes.

38. **resistance.** Base words that end in consonant + consonant combinations do not change when adding suffixes.

39. **eagerness.** When a base word ends in a consonant and a suffix begins with a consonant, you can usually attach them without changing either.

40. **crazily.** Words that end in consonant + -*y* change the -*y* to an *i* when adding suffixes.

Plurals

Plurals are a common source of spelling mistakes. For rules on making singular words into plurals, see Chapter 7.

41. **moose.** *Moose* is one of those rare words that does not change when it is pluralized. You might see one moose, or you might see several moose. You would never see mooses or meese!

42. **boundaries.** For many words ending in -*y*, the plural is made by changing the -*y* to an *i* and adding -*es* The plural of *boundary* is no exception.

43. **boxes.** Most words that end in *x* add an -*es* when becoming plural.

44. **knives.** With a few exceptions, words that end in -*f* or -*fe* will have plurals that end in -*ves*.

45. **geese.** The word *goose* is one of those strange words in the English language that has its own rules for pluralization.

46. **volcanoes** or **volcanos.** As mentioned in the introduction, some words that end in *-o* can be spelled a few different ways. The plural of *volcano* is one of these words.

47. **babies.** Like *boundary*, you drop the *-y* in *baby* and add an *-ies* to make it plural.

48. **selves.** To make the word *self* plural, replace the *-f* with a *v* and add *-es*.

49. **hatches.** Words that end in the letter *-h* will always add an *-es* when becoming plural.

50. **books.** Yes, there are still some words that just add a good ol' *-s* to become plural.

Verb Conjugations

Verb conjugations can cause a lot of problems for spellers, because there are a lot of irregular verbs that don't follow the normal rules. Once you learn the irregular verbs, however, the spelling part should be relatively easy. You can read more about verb conjugations in Chapter 8.

51. **falling/fell/fallen.** *Fall* is an irregular verb with unique past tense and past participle forms.

52. **trying/tried/tried.** *Try* is a regular verb. Remember to change the final *y* to an *i* when adding suffixes that begin with vowels.

53. **marrying/married/married.** *Marry* is a regular verb. Remember to change the final *y* to an *i* when adding suffixes that begin with vowels.

54. **expecting/expected/expected.** *Expect* is a regular verb that adds *-ing* and *-ed* endings with no change to the base word.

55. **cutting/cut/cut.** *Cut* is an irregular verb that does not change between the present tense, past tense, and past participle forms.

56. **making/made/made.** *Make* is an irregular verb that has the same past tense and past participle form.

57. **comparing/compared/compared.** *Compare* is a regular verb. Remember to drop the silent *e* when adding suffixes that begin with vowels to words that end in silent *e*.

58. **laying/laid/lain.** *Lay* is an irregular verb with unique past tense and past participle forms.

59. **breaking/broke/broken.** *Break* is an irregular verb with unique past tense and past participle forms.

60. **catching/caught/caught.** *Catch* is an irregular verb that has the same past tense and past participle form.

Rule the Rules
Smart Strategies for Star Spellers

Sometimes in life, it can feel like there are just too many rules to follow. There are rules telling us where we can go, what we can do, and how we should behave. There are rules that are strictly enforced, and rules that can sometimes be ignored. We have different rules at home than we do at school or at work, and still other rules for everywhere else. It can be hard to remember all the rules we're supposed to follow just to get through the day!

Many people feel this way about spelling. There are lots of rules to remember, and these rules are not always consistent. If you read the pretest answers, for example, you might have learned about a famous mnemonic that says, "*i* before *e*, except after *c*." This means that in most words that have the letters *i* and *e* grouped together, the *i* will come before the *e*, unless there is a *c* immediately before this combination. So, for instance, in the word *piece*, the *i* comes before the *e*, and in the word *receipt*, the *e* comes before the *i*.

FUEL FOR THOUGHT

A **mnemonic**–pronounced (ñ-mŏn′ĭk)–is a phrase or rhyme that is used to make memorization easier. You have probably heard the following mnemonic, which is used to remember how many days are in each month:

> *Thirty days has September*
> *April, June, and November*
> *All the rest have 31*
> *Except for February alone.*

Another well-known mnemonic is Roy G. Biv, which stands for the order of colors in a rainbow: red, orange, yellow, green, blue, indigo, violet.

Mnemonics can be very helpful when it comes to remembering spelling rules. If there aren't any mnemonics for words that you frequently misspell, feel free to show your creativity and make up your own!

The "i before e, except after c" rule works very nicely for most i and e words such as *thief*, *believe*, and *conceive*. But, there are words like *beige* and *concierge* that refuse to obey the rule. This is because the "i before e" rule applies only to words in which i and e combine to form a long e sound. If e and i form a long a sound, as in *beige*, *vein*, or *weigh*, the e comes before the i. (An amended version of the rhyme that many people use reads: "i before e, except after c, or when sounding like a as in *neighbor* and *weigh*.") *Concierge*, on the other hand, is a French word that is spelled according to French rules, not English rules. So right there, already, we have three different rules to remember—for just two letters!

After reading this example, it might feel like improving your spelling is too much hard work. Don't lose heart! There are always exceptions to the rules, but the exceptions are a pretty small percentage of words. If you read this book closely and do the practice exercises and puzzles, you will learn the rules that will help you spell the majority of words. Once you have a good grasp of the basic rules, you will find it much easier to remember the exceptions as well.

PRACTICE LAP

Mark whether each of the following words is spelled correctly or incorrectly.

Word	Correct	Incorrect
1. sliegh	_____	_____
2. receive	_____	_____
3. acheive	_____	_____
4. grief	_____	_____
5. frieght	_____	_____

Check your answers at the end of the chapter. How did you do?

LISTENING TO LETTERS

Now that you're thoroughly terrified with all this talk of endless rules and exceptions that must be memorized, let's take a look at the most basic, most easily remembered rule of them all, which will work in an incredible number of circumstances: *Sound the words out.*

Anyone who can read and write is already familiar with the process of sounding words out. Once children have learned to recognize the letters of the alphabet, the next thing they are taught is the sound each letter makes. You may remember studying phonics when you were younger. With phonics, you learned to connect letter patterns to the sounds they represent. Later, you learned how to break words down into syllables. Nowadays, this process has probably become automatic for you, but you still use it every time you encounter an unfamiliar word. For example, take a look at this word:

    intemperate (unrestrained)

You may have never seen this word before, but just by knowing the basic rules of phonics and syllabication, you can probably figure out how to pronounce it. You've seen the prefix before in words like *invisible* and *inside*. The second syllable, *-temp-*, is pronounced just as it would be in *temper* or *temperature*. The third syllable, *-er-*, is pronounced just as it looks, and the suffix, *-ate*, is pronounced as it would be in words like *moderate* and *passionate*. Taken all together, you can figure out that *intemperate* is pronounced (ĭn-tĕmp′ər-ĭt).

CAUTION!

THE "OFFICIAL" PRONUNCIATION of a word is not always the same as the conversational pronunciation. Slang usage and accents often change the way words are used when they're spoken out loud. For example, some people pronounce the word *aunt* as *ant*, while others pronounce it as *ahnt*. Both pronunciations are perfectly acceptable; however, if you are one of those people who says *ant*, you will have no indication when you sound the word out that there is a *u* after the *a*. Be careful of words like this; differing pronunciations can sometimes lead to mistakes in spelling.

Another example is the letter *g* in words that end in *-ing*. It is common in conversation to drop the letter *g*, so a word like *running* becomes *runnin*, or *saying* becomes *sayin*. If you use these words in conversation, people will know what you mean and they probably will not correct you. If you spell them the way you pronounce them, however, it will count against you.

HOW TO RĒD PRƏ-NŬN'SĒ-Ā'SHƏN CHÄRTZ

In almost any dictionary, immediately following each word, you will find a strange sort of code. Look up the word *dictionary*, for instance, and you might find a lis ting that looks like this:

dictionary (dĭk'shə-nair'ē) *n*: a reference guide containing an alphabetical list of words, including information relating to definition, pronunciation, and etymology

The code that follows the word explains how to pronounce that word. This is called a pronunciation guide. Most of the letters are immediately recognizable—*d*, *k*, *sh*, *n*, *a*, *i*, and *r*. Other letters look familiar but have strange symbols above them—ĭ and ē. One letter looks like it was dropped to earth from an alien spacecraft—ə.

FUEL FOR THOUGHT

THE INTERNATIONAL PHONETIC Association was formed in 1866 with the goal of creating a distinct symbol for every sound used in human language. The alphabet they created was called the International Phonetic Alphabet (IPA). This alphabet uses Latin and Greek letters to stand for common sounds. Today, there are 107 letters used for consonants and vowels and a number of marks and symbols used to give further information about these letters.

Although the IPA is an internationally recognized system, most dictionaries use a simplified form of it in their pronunciation guides. The IPA can be difficult to understand for people who have not seen it before. For instance, in IPA, the word *uncle* is written ('ʌnkəl). Someone who was trained in languages could look at those symbols and know exactly how the word was pronounced, but it is not very practical for the average reader. Most dictionaries use a combination of IPA characters and ordinary letters to make it easier for their users. The downside of this compromise is that pronunciation guides change from dictionary to dictionary; so if you want to know how to pronounce an unfamiliar word, you'll still probably have to start by learning how your dictionary works!

The pronunciation guide is mostly necessary for vowels. Most consonants have one pronunciation that is always the same; for example, the letter *d* is always pronounced *duh*. There are some exceptions, of course—*c* can be pronounced as an *s* or as a *k*—but for the most part, consonants are constant (try to say that three times fast!).

Pronunciation guides also typically show which syllable should be stressed. In this book, the accent is designated with an apostrophe. In the word *broken*, for instance, the first syllable is stressed. So the pronunciation would be written (brōk'ən).

The following chart lists the pronunciation symbols used in this book. You can also find this chart in Appendix C for quick reference.

ă	a as in **apple**	n	n as in f**u**n
ā	a as in **ace**	ŏ	o as in m**o**p
ä	a as in st**ar**	ō	o as in t**oe**
âr	ar as in c**are**	ô	o as in t**orn**, a as in w**arm**, aw as in **aw**kward
ə	a as in **a**bout, e as in th**e**, i as in penc**i**l, o as in bish**o**p, u as in s**u**pply	oi	oi as in n**oi**se, oy as in b**oy**
b	b as in **b**aby	ŏŏ	oo as in f**oo**t, u as in p**u**t
ch	ch as in **ch**icken	ow	ou as in **ou**t
d	d as in **d**og	p	p as in **p**in
ĕ	e as in b**e**t	r	r as in **r**eal
ē	e as in compl**e**te, y as in hungr**y**	s	s as in me**ss**, c as in **c**ity
ər	er as in butt**er**, ir as in b**ir**d, or as in doct**or**, ur as in **ur**ge	t	t as in **t**iny
f	f as in **f**ast, ph as in **ph**one	th	th as in **th**in
g	g as in **g**ood	*th*	th as in **th**e
h	h as in **h**at	ŭ	u as in r**u**n, o as in h**o**ney
ĭ	i as in h**i**m	ū	u as in **u**niform
îr	ier as in p**ier**, ear as in f**ear**	ü	oo as in b**oo**t

ī	i as in **i**ce	yû	u as in **c**ure, **c**ute
j	j as in **j**ob	v	v as in **v**isit
k	k as in **k**id, c as in **c**ookie	w	w as in **w**hy
l	l as in **l**ie, le as in beet**le**	z	z as in **z**ombie
m	m as in **m**an	zh	si as in vi**si**on, ge as in gara**ge**

PRACTICE LAP

Using the pronunciation guide as reference, spell the following words.

Pronunciation   **Word**

6. (ə-fĕk′shən)   _____

7. (hôr′ə-bəl)   _____

8. (kŭm-yû′nĭ-kāt)   _____

9. (ə-băn-dən)   _____

10. (ŏb′vē-əs)   _____

Check your answers at the end of the chapter. How did you do?

MEAN WHAT YOU SAY

The 2002 documentary *Spellbound* followed a group of students who were preparing for the National Spelling Bee championship in Washington, D.C. Most of the students spent weeks and months before the competition memorizing long lists of difficult-to-spell words. When asked to define some of the words on their lists, the students drew a blank. After all, they were in the National Spelling Bee, not the National Definition Bee!

Memorizing vast lists of unknown words is a great idea if you're trying to become the world's best speller, but it is not an incredibly useful skill in everyday life. You should know the meaning of the words you're using, and if you don't, you should take the time to look them up in a dictionary.

Often, if you can attach meaning to a word, this makes it easier to remember how to spell it. In addition, the homonyms and commonly confused words mentioned in Chapter 2 will become much easier to distinguish once you know their meanings.

PRACTICE LAP

Use a dictionary to look up the definitions of the italicized words, then circle the word that best fits the sentence.

11. Our school sold donated gifts in a charity (*auction/action*) to raise money for the new gym.

12. Mikey didn't like to lie because it troubled his (*conscious/conscience*).

13. Amanda (*opposed/composed*) and performed a beautiful song for the school's talent show.

14. Mr. Jacoby was on a diet, so he (*declined/inclined*) to order dessert.

15. In the American justice system, one is (*presumed/resumed*) innocent until proven guilty.

Check your answers at the end of the chapter. How did you do?

RESEARCH, RESEARCH, RESEARCH

Books like this one are a great resource for spelling tips and quizzes. Many other excellent resources can be found for free on the Internet. Some sites that might help you with your spelling and vocabulary development are:

➡ **www.dictionary.com:** Featuring definitions from several different dictionaries, as well as a word-of-the-day, daily word puzzles, and links to other word reference sources, dictionary.com is a great site to add to your permanent bookmarks.

- **www.merriam-webster.com:** Merriam Webster Online is a great source for interesting facts about words, as well as a useful online dictionary. Word games and a daily podcast help make learning fun.
- **www.myspellit.com:** Another Merriam-Webster website, Spell It! contains a downloadable list of words featured in the national spelling bee.
- **www.spellingbee.com:** The Scripps Howard National Spelling Bee site contains "Carolyn's Corner" with weekly tips and information on spelling.
- **owlenglish.purdue.edu:** Sponsored by Purdue University, the Purdue Online Writing Lab (OWL, get it?) is one of the best online resources for grammar and writing questions.
- **www.say-it-in-english.com/spellhome.html:** A concise guide to many of the topics covered in this book.
- **literacy.kent.edu/midwest/materials/ndakota/spelling/toc.html:** It's worth taking the time to type in the URL on this one! This site contains a number of useful spelling lessons and practice exercises.
- **www.spellweb.com:** Type in a word and this site will tell you whether or not it is spelled correctly.
- **www.wsu.edu/~brians/errors/index.html:** Paul Brians's "Common Errors in English" site contains an extensive list of common errors in the English language that can help you avoid spelling mistakes.

CROSSING THE FINISH LINE

In this chapter, you learned that mnemonics are phrases or rhymes used to make memorization easier. One well-known spelling mnemonic is "*i* before *e*, except after *c*, or when sounding like *a* as in *neighbor* and *weigh*." You learned that it can be useful to sound words out when unsure of their spelling; however, be careful of slang and regional pronunciations of words. We learned a little about pronunciation charts, as well as the International Phonetic Alphabet. Finally, you learned about a number of websites that provide valuable spelling, grammar, and vocabulary resources.

GAME TIME: SEARCH-A-WORD

The following sentences contain 28 misspelled words from the Chapter 1 word list. First, determine which words are spelled incorrectly, and write the correct versions in the blanks below the sentences. Then, find and circle these words in the puzzle. The words can be found vertically, horizontally, diagonally, backward, or forward. You'll find the solution at the end of the chapter. Happy hunting!

1. The hotel conseirge deklined to comunicate her afection for her job.

2. When I was in the hospital, I had a lot of greif every time the doctor stuck another needle into my vien.

3. As our sliegh raced through the horible snowstorm, Victoria com-mposed a nemonic ode to the intemprat weather.

4. I can't wait to recieve the baige basket I won at the awktion.

5. The gym teacher persumed I was oposed to exercise because I wiegh more than I once did.

6. The store owner took legal aktion against the theif who stole the peice of candy.

7. I couldn't concieve of how to acheive the desired results, but my conshence told me to beleive that things would turn out all right.

8. The freiht train resoomed its long trek.

9. The answers to the fonics test were ovious to me.

Misspelled Words:

_____   _____   _____   _____

_____   _____   _____   _____

H	E	A	D	B	F	D	E	S	O	P	P	O	A	O	Y
O	N	V	O	E	K	U	T	U	A	G	L	N	J	Z	Q
R	G	N	O	I	T	C	A	O	R	B	J	Q	I	R	U
R	E	M	H	G	C	I	R	I	P	E	T	K	P	E	K
I	T	S	B	E	L	I	E	V	E	V	R	H	H	C	V
B	U	W	U	S	W	F	P	B	C	E	G	T	O	E	L
L	V	B	D	M	N	E	M	O	N	I	C	H	R	I	E
E	P	I	E	C	E	B	E	A	E	H	T	G	R	V	G
D	G	W	S	V	D	D	T	W	I	C	I	I	I	E	R
E	E	C	O	M	M	U	N	I	C	A	T	E	B	Z	E
N	N	C	P	H	O	N	I	C	S	X	C	R	L	N	I
I	O	R	M	G	D	C	Q	S	N	N	S	F	E	L	C
L	P	N	O	I	T	C	U	A	O	E	H	A	H	Y	N
C	E	D	C	E	Y	E	F	C	C	M	R	E	M	F	O
E	X	P	F	L	A	F	F	E	C	T	I	O	N	J	C
D	E	M	U	S	E	R	P	R	I	T	H	I	E	F	G

CHAPTER 1 WORD LIST

abandon (ə-ban´dŭn)

achieve (ə-chēv´)

action (ak´shŭn)

affection (ə-fek´shŭn)

auction (ôk´shŭn)

beige (bāzh)

believe (bē-lēv´)

communicate (kŭm-yü´ni-kāt)

composed (kŭm´pōsd)

conceive (kŭn-sēv´)

concierge (kon-sē´ârzh)

conscience (kon´zhins)

conscious (kon´zhŭs)

declined (dē-klīnd)

freight (frāt)

grief (grēf)

horrible (hôr´ə-bəl)

inclined (in´klīnd)

intemperate (in-temp´ ər-it)

mnemonic (nĭ-mŏn´ĭk)

obvious (ob´vē-ŭs)

opposed (ə´pōsd)

phonics (fo´niks)

piece (pēs)

presumed (prē-sümd´)

receipt (rē-sēt´)

receive (rē-sēv´)

resumed (rē-sümd´)

sleigh (slā)

thief (thēf)

vein (vān)

weigh (wā)

ANSWERS

1. **incorrect.** When the letters *e* and *i* combine to make a long *a* sound, the *e* almost always comes first. The correct spelling of this word is *sleigh*.

2. **correct.** This word follows the rule "*i* before *e*, except after *c*."

3. **incorrect.** This word also follows the "*i* before *e*, except after *c*" rule. Although this word has a *c* before the *i* and *e*, remember that the *c* must come *immediately* before the *i* and *e* in order for the rule to apply. The correct spelling of this word is *achieve*.

4. **correct.** Once again, this word follows the "*i* before *e*, except after *c*" rule. There is no *c* in this word, so *grief* is the correct spelling.

5. **incorrect.** In this word, the letters *e* and *i* combine to make a long *a* sound. The correct spelling of this word is *freight*.

6. **affection.** The trickiest thing about this word is remembering what sound the ə symbol represents. Remember: ə is used to stand for the *a* sound in words like *about* and *among*.

7. **horrible.** This one isn't too tricky . . . remember that ô is the *o* sound in words like *torn* and *corn*.

8. **communicate.** This one looks quite different from the actual spelling of the word, but it's not too hard to figure out if you read closely. Remember that *c* will always be represented by a *k* or an *s* in pronunciation guides.

9. **abandon.** Again, the ə symbol is the key to understanding this word.

10. **obvious.** The most difficult thing about this word is remembering that ē represents a long *e* sound. Long vowels are always marked by a horizontal line, which is known as a macron.

11. **auction.** An *auction* is a sale in which goods or services are sold to the highest bidder, while *action* is the process of doing something.

12. **conscience.** The *conscience* is an inner sense of right and wrong. Although it shares the same root as the word *conscious*, *conscience* is a noun, while *conscious* is an adjective; in this case, *conscience* is the correct word.

13. **composed.** To *oppose* something is to be against it, while to *compose* something is to write or create it. *Composed* is the correct word in this case.

14. **declined.** Someone on a diet would *decline* dessert, or refuse it.

15. presumed. To *resume* means to continue. To *presume* means to assume. People in America are *assumed* to be innocent until proven guilty, so *presumed* is the correct word in this situation.

Game Time: Search-A-Word Solution

Misspelled Words:

concierge
declined
communicate
affection
grief
vein
sleigh
horrible (appears twice)
composed
mnemonic

intemperate
receive
beige
auction
presumed
opposed
weigh
action
thief
piece

conceive
achieve
conscience
believe
freight
resumed
phonics
obvious

H	E	A	D	B	F	D	E	S	O	P	P	O	A	O	Y
O	N	V	O	E	K	U	T	U	A	G	L	N	J	Z	Q
R	G	N	O	I	T	C	A	O	R	B	J	Q	I	R	U
R	E	M	H	G	C	I	R	I	P	E	T	K	P	E	K
I	T	S	B	E	L	I	E	V	E	V	R	H	H	C	V
B	U	W	U	S	W	F	P	B	C	E	G	T	O	E	L
L	V	B	D	M	N	E	M	O	N	I	C	H	R	I	E
E	P	I	E	C	E	B	E	A	E	H	T	G	R	V	G
D	G	W	S	V	D	D	T	W	I	C	I	I	I	E	R
E	E	C	O	M	M	U	N	I	C	A	T	E	B	Z	E
N	N	C	P	H	O	N	I	C	S	X	C	R	L	N	I
I	O	R	M	G	D	C	Q	S	N	N	S	F	E	L	C
L	P	N	O	I	T	C	U	A	O	E	H	A	H	Y	N
C	E	D	C	E	Y	E	F	C	C	M	R	E	M	F	O
E	X	P	F	L	A	F	F	E	C	T	I	O	N	J	C
D	E	M	U	S	E	R	P	R	I	T	H	I	E	F	G

Which Word Is Which?
Homonyms and Commonly Confused Words

The first types of errors we're going to explore are actually not spelling mistakes at all—they're vocabulary mistakes. Take a look at the following sentences.

Sarah and Jane left *they're* workbooks at school.

I put my shoes over *their*.

There going to visit Grandma sometime next month.

What is wrong with the italicized words in these sentences? It's not that the words have been misspelled. In each example, the italicized word is spelled correctly; it has just been used incorrectly.

Words like *there*, *their*, and *they're* are called **homonyms**—words that have the same pronunciation but different meanings. It is easy to confuse homonyms, even if you know exactly what they mean. Even the best writers confuse the words *there*, *their*, and *they're* from time to time. More often than not, the confusion comes from simple carelessness. The best way to avoid making mistakes with homonyms is to learn how each word is used and then double-check your work carefully.

INSIDE TRACK

HOMONYMS (hŏ′mə-nĭmz) are words that are pronounced the same but have different meanings, or words that are spelled identically but have different pronunciations and definitions.

The word *homonym* actually refers to two different terms—*homophone* and *homograph*.

Homophones (hŏ′mə-fōnz) are words that are spelled differently but have the same pronunciation and different meanings. *Pear*, meaning "a kind of fruit," and *pare*, meaning "to cut," are homophones.

Homographs (hŏ′mə-grăfs) are words that have an identical spelling to other words but have a different meaning and different pronunciation. For example, *sewer* (sü′ər), meaning "a place for waste," and *sewer* (sō′ər), meaning "one who sews," are homographs.

People often use the word *homonym* to mean *homophone*—that is, words that are pronounced the same but have different definitions, like *pear* and *pare*. However, be aware that homographs are considered homonyms, as well.

The word *they're* is probably the easiest to remember, because it looks different from the other two. *They're* is a contraction meaning "they are." If you need to know whether or not *they're* is the correct word to use, simply substitute the words *they are* in the sentence. For example, take another look at the first sentence:

Sarah and Jane left *they're* workbooks at school.

If you substituted for the contraction, the sentence above would read "Sarah and Jane left *they are* workbooks at school." This does not make any sense, so you know that in this sentence, the correct word will be either *there* or *their*.

But which one? *Their* means "belonging to them," while *there* means "that place." To find the correct word, you have to first determine what the sentence is trying to say. In this case, we can figure out from the sentence that the workbooks belong to Sarah and Jane; therefore, the correct word for this sentence is *their*.

If you frequently confuse the words *their*, *there*, and *they're*, this would be a great situation to create a mnemonic. Remember: Mnemonics can be anything that helps you remember how to spell words, not necessarily just rhymes. You could use the sentence "**The ir**on is **their**s" to remember that "belonging to them" is spelled *the* + *ir*. You could remember *there* with the sentence "**There** is not **here**," and for *they're*, you could say, "In *they are*, the *a* stands for *apostrophe*."

PRACTICE LAP

Fill in the following blanks with either *there*, *their*, or *they're*.

1. The Ambersons are having _____ annual holiday party tonight.

2. Are you staying here or going _____?

3. The rock band had _____ first hit in 2005.

4. _____ happy that we came to _____ restaurant.

5. The first time I saw _____ new puppy, I knew he belonged _____.

Check your answers at the end of the chapter. How did you do?

COMMON HOMONYMS

There are hundreds of homonym pairs in the English language. The following table lists some of the more commonly confused homonym pairs.

Homonym	Brief Definition
allowed	permitted
aloud	spoken
bare (verb)	to show
bear (verb)	to withstand

Homonym	Brief Definition
beat	to hit
beet	red vegetable
board	a piece of wood
bored	uninterested
bough	tree branch
bow	to bend in a sign of respect
brake	device that stops a car or bike
break	to split apart
capital	most important
capitol	government building
cell	a small room, as in a jail
sell	to trade for money
cite	to refer to
sight	vision
site	a location
coarse	rough
course	path
complement	match
compliment	praise
council	group of leaders
counsel	attorney, advisor
dear	beloved
deer	forest animal with antlers

Homonym	Brief Definition
die	to no longer live
dye	a substance that creates color
dual	double
duel	sword fight
elicit	to draw out
illicit	against the law
fair	considering all sides
fare	payment for travel or admittance
feat	accomplishment
feet	the things you walk on
find	locate
fined	made to pay a penalty
foreword	an introduction to a book
forward	to the front
gait	the way one walks or runs
gate	a door on a fence
grate	a frame used as a covering
great	excellent
heal	to cure
heel	the back of the foot
incite	to provoke
insight	ability to understand

Homonym	Brief Definition
lead	metal
led	guided
loan	let borrow
lone	single
overdo	do too much
overdue	late payment
pain	ache
pane	a panel of glass
passed	moved beyond
past	time before the present
peace	the opposite of war
piece	a small part of
peal	ring
peel	the outer shell of fruit
pedal	device operated by the foot
peddle	to sell
peer	equal
pier	landing place for ships
plain	humble
plane	flying machine
principal (adjective)	main
principal (noun)	person in charge
principle	standard, moral

Homonym	Brief Definition
rain	state of weather
reign	rule
rein	rope used for steering a horse
right	correct
rite	ritual
wright	one who makes something
write	compose, as language
soar	fly
sore	in pain
stationary	still, not moving
stationery	writing paper
tail	hindmost appendage on an animal
tale	story
team	a group working together
teem	to be filled with
vain	having a large ego
vein	blood vessel
vary	to change
very	extremely
waist	area of the body above the hips
waste	misuse
who's	contraction meaning "who is"
whose	belonging to someone

CHOOSING BETWEEN HOMONYMS

When trying to choose between homonyms, sentence clues can help quite a bit. Take, for example, the words *weak* and *week*. This is a simple example, because you should already know the difference between these words. *Weak* is an adjective meaning "not strong," while *week* is a noun meaning the seven-day period that begins on Sunday and ends on Saturday.

I chose these words to show how you can use parts of speech to determine which word belongs in a blank. For example, read the following sentence:

The swami felt (*weak/week*) after seven days of fasting.

In this example, you don't need to know that a swami is a Hindu religious leader or that fasting means "to not eat for an extended period of time, often for religious reasons." Don't even worry about the "seven days" part . . . that's just in there to trick you. The important thing to look at here is where the word is positioned in the sentence.

In this case, the word immediately follows the verb, *felt*. *Felt* is a sensory verb and *sensory verbs are always followed by an adjective*. Without understanding anything else in the sentence, you can determine that the correct word choice in this sentence is the adjective, *weak*.

INSIDE TRACK

SENSORY VERBS are verbs that are related to the senses—touch, taste, smell, sound, and sight. (*Seem* and *appear* are also considered sensory verbs.) In a sentence that uses a sensory verb, the adjective will always directly follow the verb and describe the subject. Here are a few examples:

➡ You look ridiculous. (*Look* is a sensory verb; *ridiculous* is an adjective that describes the subject, *you*.)

➡ The television seems broken. (*Seems* is a sensory verb; *broken* is an adjective that describes the subject, *television*.)

➡ Dinner smells really delicious! (*Smells* is a sensory verb; *delicious* is an adjective that describes the subject, *dinner*. *Really* is an adverb that describes the adjective, *delicious*.)

In situations in which the homonyms are each the same part of speech, it is often enough to understand the meaning of only one of the words. For example, the words *team* and *teem* are a homonym pair that are commonly used on standardized tests. You probably already know that *team* is a noun meaning "organized group," as in a baseball team or a team of lawyers. *Team* can also be used as a verb. For example, you could say:

> Every year, our school *teams* with the local television station to collect canned food for needy families.

The verb *teams* means "joins with, or unites."

The word *teem* is also a verb. Now which word fits best in the following sentence?

> During lunchtime, the cafeteria (*teams/teems*) with hungry students.

The correct answer is *teems*, which means "filled with." If you did not know the definition of the word *teems*, you could still pick it as the correct answer based on your knowledge of the word *teams*. The cafeteria is more likely to be full of hungry students than to join with hungry students.

PRACTICE LAP

In the following, use your knowledge of sentence structure and word definitions to choose the italicized word that best fits the sentence.

6. The threat of a potential storm made me feel (*tense/tents*) all day.

7. We're taking a helicopter ride that (*soars/sores*) over the Grand Canyon.

8. Once you've hooked a fish, you have to wind the line to (*real/reel*) it in.

9. You should (*mince/mints*) the celery into tiny pieces before adding it to the stew.

10. We began our (*ascent/assent*) at the foot of the hill.

Check your answers at the end of the chapter. How did you do?

COMMONLY CONFUSED WORDS

Commonly confused words are words that are not necessarily homonyms but are often mistaken for one another. *Accept* and *except* are commonly confused words, as are *assure, ensure,* and *insure, farther* and *further,* and *loose* and *lose.* The following list shows some of the most commonly confused word pairs, along with a brief definition of each word.

Confusing Words	Brief Definition
accept	recognize
except	excluding
access	means of approaching
excess	extra
adapt	to adjust
adopt	to take as one's own
affect	to influence
effect (noun)	result
effect (verb)	to bring about
all ready	totally prepared
already	by this time
among	in the middle of several
between	in an interval separating (two)
assure	to make someone feel confident
ensure	to make certain
insure	to guarantee against loss or harm
beside	next to
besides	in addition to
breath (noun)	a single cycle of inhalation and exhalation
breathe (verb)	to inhale and exhale
breadth	width

Confusing Words	Brief Definition
disinterested	no strong opinion either way
uninterested	unengaged; having no interest in
envelop	surround
envelope	paper container for a letter
farther	beyond
further	additional
loose	not tight
lose	unable to find
may be	is a possibility
maybe	perhaps
personal	individual
personnel	employees
precede	go before
proceed	continue
proceeds	profits
than	in contrast to
then	next in time
who	substitute for he, she, or they
whom	substitute for him, her, or them

THE KINGS OF CONFUSION

Some of the commonly confused words you just read are very different in definition. It should be easy to remember that the only instance in which you spell the word *capitol* with an *o* is when you are referring to a governmental building; in every other instance, the word is spelled with an *a*.

Some of the words aren't that easy, however. Following are explanations of the more confusing cases.

accept/except

Accept and *except* are both very common words, and many people have trouble remembering when to use each. Take a look at how the two words are used in the following sentences:

> Everyone *except* George is prepared to *accept* the final results of the vote.

As the sample sentence shows, *accept* is commonly used as a verb, while *except* is commonly used in the same way as the word *but*.

Except can also be used as a verb, but its usage is very different from *accept*. The verb form of *except* means "to exclude." For example, you might say:

> *Except*ing George, we were all prepared to *accept* the final results of the vote.

When choosing between *except* and *accept*, the first thing you should do is decide which part of speech the word needs to be. If the required word should be a verb, chances are strong that the best choice will be *accept*. The only time in which *except* will be used as a verb is when it indicates that someone or something is being excluded. If the required word is *not* a verb, the correct word will always be *except*.

affect/effect

One of the most commonly confused word pairs is *affect* and *effect*. The words are often confused because they not only sound similar, but also have similar meanings. Just remember:

If the word is a noun, it is probably effect. An *effect* is a result. It is often used in variations of the phrase *to have an effect* or *to have no effect*. For example, you could say:

John's speech had a powerful *effect* on the way I think about recycling.

Or:

I keep trying to teach my dog how to roll over, to no *effect*.

Technically, *affect* can also be used as a noun, but its meaning is so specific and obscure that it is rarely used. The noun *affect* means emotion, as distinguished from thought or action. Its usage is so uncommon, in fact, that I'm not even going to provide you with a sample sentence. Just remember: If the word is a noun, 99.9% of the time, *effect* will be the correct choice.

If the word is a verb, it is probably *affect*. To *affect* something means "to have an influence on." For example, you could say:

The moon *affects* the tides.

Or:

My grades were *affected* positively when I started going to sleep an hour earlier.

Effect can be used as a verb, but its usage is much less common. *Effect* as a verb means "to produce a result," as in the sentence, "Teachers try hard to *effect* changes on their students." Although this sentence is grammatically correct, more often than not, if the sentence calls for a verb, *affect* will be the correct choice.

assure/ensure/insure

Assure, ensure, and *insure* are all verbs with a similar meaning, which might lead you to believe that this means the words are interchangeable. You didn't really think it would be that easy, did you? Their meanings may be similar, but each word is used in very distinct situations.

Assure means "to make someone feel confident about something." An assurance is something one person does for another person. If you were out late at night, for example, you would call your parents to *assure* them that you would be home in time for curfew. You might *assure* your friend that you will pay her back the $5 you borrowed from her, even if you have no intention of doing such a thing.

Ensure means "to make certain that something will happen." You would *ensure* that you'd get home in time for curfew by leaving a few minutes early. You could also *ensure* that you brought enough warm clothes on vacation by packing your own bags.

Insure means "to guarantee against loss or harm." It is a financial term that is used with things like health insurance or life insurance. If you were an adult, you could *insure* your house against fire.

Be careful! People often write *insure* when they actually mean *ensure*. Unless you're discussing healthcare or financial information, it's a pretty safe bet that *ensure* is the word you should use.

farther/further

Even the finest authors in the world (like the writer of this book, for instance) sometimes get the words *farther* and *further* confused. *Farther* and *further* are comparison words. The difference is that *farther* refers only to physical distance, while *further* refers to a relationship between two points, as in time. For example, you would say that one house is *farther* down the road than another, but you would be *further* along in a book than someone else. You can never physically go *further*; you must go *farther*. If you are referring to actual distance, *farther* is the correct word; in all other situations, *further* is correct.

loose/lose

There's no real reason why these two words should be confused, but they often are. They don't sound anything alike, they're totally different parts of speech, and they mean completely different things. Just remember: Something that isn't tight is *loose*. You *lose* something when you can't find it. *Loose* is an adjective, and *lose* is a verb. Enough said!

than/then

Than is used to compare two things. You might say that you're smarter *than* your brother or that you like pizza better *than* spaghetti. *Then*, on the other hand, is used when referring to time. You could say, "We went to the store. *Then* we returned home." Or you could say, "If our teacher is ill, *then* we will have a substitute." Although the two words are spelled similarly, they are used to mean very different things.

PRACTICE LAP

Decide which commonly confused word belongs in each of the following sentences.

11. Ms. Richards said she will still (*accept/except*) my social studies assignment, even though it's late.

12. The overwhelming smell of paint in the room made it difficult to (*breath/breathe*).

13. (*Who/Whom*) might I say is calling?

14. If you enjoy singing more (*than/then*) dancing, (*than/then*) you should quit the pompom squad and join the choir.

15. When giving a speech, it is important to thank the speaker who (*preceded/proceeded*) you.

Check your answers at the end of the chapter. How did you do?

CROSSING THE FINISH LINE

We learned in this chapter that many spelling mistakes are actually vocabulary mistakes. *They're*, *their*, and *there* are examples of commonly confused homonyms—words that have the same pronunciation but different meanings or words that are spelled identically but have different pronunciations and definitions. When trying to find the correct homonym for a sentence, look closely at sentence clues. First, check to find the word's part of speech. If the homonyms have the same part of speech, sometimes one word can be eliminated based on definition.

> **FUEL FOR THOUGHT**
>
> **PART OF SPEECH:** The classification of a word according to its function in context, including the noun, pronoun, verb, adjective, adverb, preposition, conjunction, and interjection, and sometimes the article.

Some words such as *accept/except*, *assure/ensure/insure*, and *farther/further* are commonly confused because of similar spellings or pronunciations. Although these words may seem similar, they often have very different meanings. Read each sentence closely to determine the italicized word that best fits it.

GAME TIME: RIDDLE ME THIS

Decide which homonym, or frequently confused word belongs in each of the following sentences. Then, write that word in the corresponding puzzle on page 46. When you're done, enter the letters in the shaded boxes into the blanks to find the answer to the riddle.

1. Please (*grate/great*) this cheese for the salad.

2. My dad's new office is being built on this (*site/cite*).

3. To (*mints/mince*) garlic, you must cut it into tiny pieces.

4. It isn't always easy to (*adopt/adapt*) to life changes.

5. The prisoner must return to his (*cell/sell*) at the end of each day.

6. The (*peals/peels*) of the church bells could be heard in the distance.

7. This tie (*compliments/complements*) your outfit nicely.

8. The judge asked if the (*counsel/council*) for the defense was ready.

9. "I challenge you to a (*dual/duel*)!" shouted the knight.

10. The weather is supposed to be (*fair/fare*) to sunny on Friday.

11. I would have taken the joke (*farther/further*), but my mom was getting irritated.

12. We're selling candy bars to get new uniforms for our soccer (*team/teem*).

13. My parents bought a (*stationery/stationary*) bicycle for our exercise room.

14. Mr. Collins has a great (*breathe/breadth*) of knowledge.

15. One (*principle/principal*) that I believe in is "do unto others as you would have them do unto you."

16. It takes a lot of (*capital/capitol*) to start a business.

17. I lie on my back and watch the birds (*sore/soar*) through the sky.

18. Jeremy had the (*write/right*) answer for number 26.

19. We weren't allowed to take any (*excess/access*) baggage on the flight.

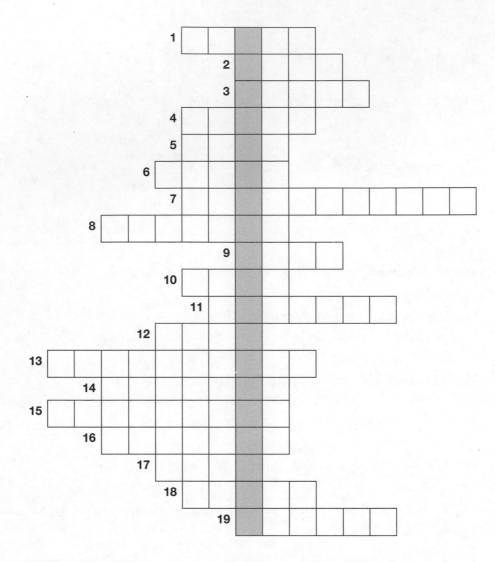

Riddle: What do you call a short psychic who is wanted by the police?

Answer: __ __ __ __ __ __ __ __ __ __ __ __ __ __

__ __ __ __ __ __ __ __

CHAPTER 2 WORD LIST

accept (ăk´sĕpt)

access (ăk´sĕs)

adapt (ə´dăpt)

adopt (ə´dŏpt)

affect (ə´fĕkt)

all ready (awl rĕd´ē)

allowed (ə-lowd´)

aloud (ə-lowd´)

already (awl rĕd´ē)

among (ə-mŭng´)

assure (ə-shûr´)

bare (bâr)

bear (bâr)

beat (bēt)

beet (bēt)

beside (bē-sīd´)

besides (bē-sīdz´)

between (bē-twēn´)

board (bôrd)

bored (bôrd)

bough (bow)

bow (bow)

brake (brāk)

breadth (brĕdth)

break (brāk)

breath (brĕth)

breathe (brē*th*)

capital (kăp´ĭ-təl)

capitol (kăp´ĭ-təl)

cell (sĕl)

cite (sīt)

coarse (kôrs)

complement (kŏm´plə-mĭnt)

compliment (kŏm´plə-mĭnt)

council (kown´səl)

counsel (kown´səl)

course (kôrs)

dear (dîr)

deer (dîr)

die (dī)

disinterested (dĭs-ĭn´trəst-əd)

dual (dül)

duel (dül)

dye (dī)

effect (ē´fĕkt)

elicit (ə-lĭs´ĭt)

ensure (ĕn-shûr´)

envelop (ĕn-vĕl´-əp)

envelope (ĕn´vəl-ōp)

except (ĕk´sĕpt)

excess (ĕk´sĕs)

fair (fâr)

fare (fâr)

farther (fâr´thər)

feat (fēt)

feet (fēt)

find (fīnd)

fined (fīnd)

foreword (fôr´wərd)

forward (fôr´wərd)

further (fər´thər)

gait (gāt)

gate (gāt)

grate (grāt)

great (grāt)

heal (hēl)

heel (hēl)

homographs (hŏ´mə-grăfs)

homonyms (hŏ´mə-nĭmz)

homophones (hŏ´mə-fōnz)

illicit (ĭl-lĭs´ĭt)

incite (ĭn-sīt)

insight (ĭn-sīt)

insure (ĭn-shûr´)

lead (lĕd)

led (lĕd)

loan (lōn)

lone (lōn)

loose (lüs)

lose (lüz)

may be (mā bē)

maybe (mā´bē)

overdo (ō-vər-dü)

overdue (ō-vər-dü)

pain (pān)

pane (pān)

passed (păsd)

past (păst)

peace (pēs)

peal (pēl)

pedal (pĕd´əl)

peddle (pĕd´əl)

peel (pēl)

peer (pêr)

personal (pər´sŭn-əl)

personnel (pər´sŭn-ĕl)

piece (pēs)

pier (pêr)

plain (plān)

plane (plān)

precede (prē-cēd´)

principal (prĭn´sĭ-pəl)

principle (prĭn´sĭ-pəl)

proceed (prō-cēd´)

proceeds (prō´cēdz)

rain (rān)

reign (rān)

rein (rān)

right (rīt)

rite (rīt)

sell (sĕl)

sigh (sī)

site (sīt)

soar (sôr)

sore (sôr)

stationary (stā'shən-âr-ē)

stationery (stā'shən-âr-ē)

tail (tāl)

tale (tāl)

team (tēm)

teem (tēm)

than (*thăn*)

then (*thĕn*)

uninterested (ŭn- ĭn'trəst-əd)

vain (vān)

vary (vâr'ē)

vein (vān)

very (vâr'ē)

waist (wāst)

waste (wāst)

who (hü)

who's (hüz)

whom (hüm)

whose (hüz)

wright (rīt)

write (rīt)

ANSWERS

1. **their.** The party was thrown by the Ambersons, so *their* is the correct answer in this sentence.
2. **there.** The word *there* means "that place." If they weren't staying *here*, they might be going *there*.
3. **their.** This sentence refers to a hit that was created by the rock band; therefore, *their* is the correct choice.
4. **They're; their.** The first blank makes sense if you fill in the words *they are*: which means *they're* is the best choice. The restaurant belongs to "them," which makes it *their* restaurant.
5. **their; there.** If the puppy belongs to them, it is *their* puppy. He belongs in a place, or *there*.

6. **tense.** To feel *tense* is to feel anxious. The word *tents* is the plural of *tent*, which is a temporary shelter. *Tense* makes much more sense in this sentence than *tents*.

7. **soars.** To *soar* is to fly. *Soar* is a verb, while *sore* is a noun. A helicopter would *soar* over the Grand Canyon.

8. **reel.** In this case, it would help to know that a *reel* is a part of a fishing pole. However, you could figure out the correct answer if you knew that *real* is an adjective, and this sentence calls for a verb.

9. **mince.** *Mints* is the plural of *mint*. To *mince* is "to cut something into tiny pieces"; therefore, *mince* is the correct choice.

10. **ascent.** To *ascend* is "to climb"; therefore, *ascent* is the correct choice.

11. **accept.** Remember that if the word is a verb, *accept* is generally the correct answer choice. *Except* is almost always used as a conjunction.

12. **breathe.** The verb form of the noun *breath* is spelled with an *e*; therefore, *breathe* is the correct choice.

13. **Who.** *Whom* is used as a substitution for *him, her,* or *them,* while *who* is used as a substitution for *he, she,* or *they.* To find the correct answer, turn the question into a statement. You would say, "I might say *he* is calling," or "I might say *they* are calling." You would not say, "I might say *them* are calling." Therefore, the correct choice is *who*.

14. **than; then.** *Than* is used when comparing two things. The first part of the sentence compares singing with dancing; therefore, *than* is the best choice. The second part of the sentence is a little trickier. The correct word is *then*, because it refers to an order in which things are done—*if* you enjoy something, *then* you should do something.

15. **preceded.** To *proceed* is to go forward. In this case, the sentence is looking for a word that means "come before." The correct choice is *preceded*.

Game Time: Riddle Me This Solution

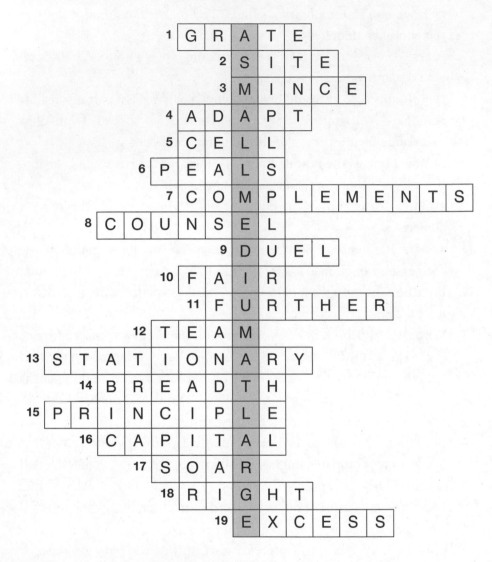

1	G	R	A	T	E						
2		S	I	T	E						
3		M	I	N	C	E					
4	A	D	A	P	T						
5	C	E	L	L							
6	P	E	A	L	S						
7	C	O	M	P	L	E	M	E	N	T	S
8	C	O	U	N	S	E	L				
9		D	U	E	L						
10	F	A	I	R							
11	F	U	R	T	H	E	R				
12	T	E	A	M							
13	S	T	A	T	I	O	N	A	R	Y	
14	B	R	E	A	D	T	H				
15	P	R	I	N	C	I	P	L	E		
16	C	A	P	I	T	A	L				
17	S	O	A	R							
18	R	I	G	H	T						
19	E	X	C	E	S	S					

Riddle: What do you call a short psychic who is wanted by the police?

Answer: A small medium at large

Building Words

If a big part of learning how to spell is learning what words mean, then a big part of learning what words mean is learning how words are put together. The words that make up the English language did not just spring, fully formed, from the mouths of people living in caves thousands of years ago. Although it's impossible to trace the development of language precisely, we do know that English has developed gradually over time, more by accident and chance than by design.

An extraordinary percentage of English words have **roots** that come from Latin or Greek words. Just as the roots of a tree give the tree a foundation, word roots establish the basic meaning of the word. Attached to the root are **affixes**, which can come before the root (**prefixes**) or after the root (**suffixes**).

FUEL FOR THOUGHT

MAKE MINE STRAWBERRY! When building an ice cream sundae, you must first decide what flavor of ice cream to use. Then you add the toppings. The ice cream determines the base flavor of the sundae, while the toppings add to or change that flavor. Some toppings, like sprinkles, just add a little extra flavor, while other toppings, like chocolate sauce, change the flavor of the entire sundae.

With words, the root is like the ice cream—it tells you what the word will be about. For example, the Latin root *vis* means "to see." The word *vis* does not exist as an English word all on its own. You can't say, "I *vis* a butterfly." Just as ice cream doesn't become a sundae until you add the toppings, most roots do not become words until you add the affixes.

The root *vis* can combine with many affixes to create many different words. If you add the suffix *-ion*, meaning "act or process," you get the word *vision*, which means "the process of seeing." You could add the suffix *-ible*, meaning "able to," to get the word *visible*, which means "able to be seen." Suffixes like *-ion* and *-ible* are similar to sprinkles on your word sundae; they don't change the meaning of the root, but they add something extra to the word's meaning.

Affixes like the prefix *in-* and the suffix *-less* are more like chocolate sauce. The prefix *in-* means "not." If you add the prefix *in-* to *visible*, you get the word *invisible*, meaning "not able to be seen." Although the root idea remains the same—to be seen—adding the prefix *in-* changes the entire meaning of the word.

Before we take a closer look at the different parts of words, let's try a few practice questions to see how much you already know.

PRACTICE LAP

Read each sentence and answer the question that follows.

1. Please *transmit* this message to my friend in France.
   Transmit means
   a. send.
   b. sell.
   c. find.
   d. mention.

2. My dad is trying to *resell* his boat.
   Resell means
   a. sell before.
   b. not sell.
   c. sell again.
   d. give away.

3. Today is the most *tranquil* day we've had this spring.
   Tranquil means
   a. stormy.
   b. peaceful.
   c. long.
   d. cold.

4. The results of the contest were *predetermined*.
   Predetermined means
   a. determined after.
   b. not determined.
   c. determined easily.
   d. determined before.

5. I thought Jack was more *amiable* than usual today.
   Amiable means
   a. friendly.
   b. tired.
   c. angry.
   d. dangerous.

Check your answers at the end of the chapter. How did you do?

BREAK IT DOWN

Before you can start to break words into roots, prefixes, and suffixes, it helps to refresh your understanding of **syllables**. Syllables are letters or combinations of letters that produce a single sound. Most syllables are somewhere between one and five letters long, and every syllable must have only one vowel sound or diphthong. (Vowel sounds are discussed in greater detail in

Chapter 4.) The word *prevented*, for example, has three syllables, each with only one vowel sound—*pre-vent-ed*. When you pronounce the word aloud, you can feel the three different breaking points in the word. In this case, each part of speech in the word gets its own syllable; *pre-* is the suffix, *vent* is the root, and *-ed* is the suffix.

Most roots, prefixes, and suffixes are either one or two syllables long, so breaking the word down into syllables is a good way to figure out which word part is which. It is important to remember, though, that words can have more than one prefix and suffix. For example, the word *unremittingly* is an adverb that means "persistently." The root of *unremittingly* is *mit*. The word has two prefixes (*un-* and *re-*) and two suffixes (*-ing* and *-ly*). Once you learn to recognize common prefixes, suffixes, and roots, you can easily take words apart to uncover their meanings.

Here are some rules to help remember where to divide syllables:

Divide between two consonants. Examples:
com / ment
fur / nish
man / ner
out / fit
con / trol

Divide after the vowel if it has a long sound. Examples:
de / light
A / pril
be / gin
ta / ble

Divide after the consonant if the vowel has a short sound. Examples:
gov / ern
gath / er
lav / ish
Aug / ust

Roots

The roots of a plant anchor the plant in the soil so that it can stand. A word root serves a similar function. Roots are the basic building blocks of all words. Every word either *is* a root or *has* a root. Just as a house cannot be built without a foundation, a word must have a root to give it meaning. Roots combine with a wide range of prefixes and suffixes to make words.

Roots can be a helpful key to understanding how to spell a word. For example, the Latin root *cred* means "believe." This is the root of the word *incredible*. Other words that share the same root are *credible*, *incredulous*, and *credit*. If you know that the root of these words is spelled *cred*, you are already well on your way to spelling all of these words.

The trickiest thing to remember about roots is that the same root can be spelled in different ways. For instance, the words *proceed*, *recede*, and *recess* all have the same root, which is commonly listed as *ced/ceed/cess*. This root means "to go, to come, or to yield." A list of common roots can be found in Appendix D.

FUEL FOR THOUGHT

THE TERMS *roots* and *base words* are sometimes used interchangeably, but they have different meanings. Roots are the basic building blocks of meaning, and they are mainly derived from Greek or Latin words. Usually, roots cannot be used as words all by themselves. *Base words*, on the other hand, are the most basic forms of words. Base words have roots, but roots do not have base words.

For example, the word *fiction* is a base word. You can add the suffix *-al* to make the adjective, *fictional*, or you can add the prefix *non-* to make the noun *nonfiction*. The most basic form of the word from which *fictional* and *nonfiction* are made is *fiction*. The *root* of fiction is *fic*, meaning "to do or to make." *Fic* is not an English word all by itself. *Fiction* is a base word, because it stands on its own as a word, and *fic* is a root, which cannot stand on its own as a word.

PRACTICE LAP

Circle the roots in the following words. Refer to Appendix D if you need help.

6. audible

7. chronic

8. exceed

9. confide

10. pedal

Check your answers at the end of the chapter. How did you do?

Prefixes and Suffixes

Prefixes and suffixes are groups of letters that connect to roots to create words. Prefixes come before the root, while suffixes come after the root. Like roots, prefixes and suffixes have a fixed meaning that remains the same, no matter which word they are attached to.

Prefixes enhance or change the meaning of a word. Although you cannot tell the meaning of a word from the prefix alone, the prefix can help you get an idea of what the word is about. The prefix *omni-*, for example, means "all." This prefix can be found in the word *omnipotent*, which means "all powerful." Now read the following sentence:

Most humans are *omnivorous* eaters.

If you recognize that the prefix *omni-* means "all," you can take a guess that this word means "all eating" . . . and you would be correct! The root *vor* means "to eat"; an *omnivorous* eater eats both plants and animals. Someone who is an *omnivorous* eater is described as an *omnivore*.

In addition to enhancing or changing the meanings of words, suffixes determine which part of speech the word will be. In the preceding sentence, for example, the word *omnivore* is a noun, while the word *omnivorous* is an adjective. The suffix *-ous* is an adjective ending, meaning "full of, having the qualities of, or relating to." You could add a second suffix to this word, *-ly*, to make the adverb *omnivorously*, as in: He eats *omnivorously*. We have just changed a noun to an adjective to an adverb, simply by changing the ending. Magic!

CAUTION!

MANY PREFIXES HAVE similar meanings, such as *dis-*, *il-*, and *un-*. Unfortunately, you cannot just substitute one word for the other willy-nilly. This is the case with the words *disable* and *unable*. *Disable* means "to cripple." Someone might *disable* the electricity before working with electrical wires, for example. *Unable*, on the other hand, means "not able." You could be *unable* to answer a phone because you were busy. You would never say that you were *disable* to answer the phone, even though both *dis-* and *un-* mean "not."

The same applies to suffixes. The adjective endings *-able* and *-ible* mean "capable of worthy of; tending or liable to." These endings can be a source of confusion in spelling, because they sound alike and there is only one letter difference between them. You cannot use them in place of one another, however; the word meaning "can be eaten" is spelled *edible*, not *edable*.

But don't lose hope just yet! There is a rule that addresses the *-ible* and *-able* dilemma. The rule is, if the word is not a complete word on its own, use *-ible*, as in *edible*, *visible*, and *incredible*. If the word can be used on its own in a sentence, add *-able*, as in *fashionable*, *comfortable*, and *bearable*. (If the word is a complete word that ends in an *-e*, drop the final *e* before adding the *-able*, as in *excusable* and *valuable*.)

There are a few exceptions to this rule, such as *reversible* and *digestible*, but the *-able/-ible* rule can help you remember how to spell many of the most common words.

PRACTICE LAP

Circle the suffixes and prefixes in the following words.

11. unlikely

12. introduce

13. revert

14. instinctual

15. amazement

16. prepare

17. counterpart

18. goodness

19. repulsive

20. cooperatively

Check your answers at the end of the chapter. How did you do?

HYPHENATED AND COMPOUND WORDS

Hyphenated words are words that are connected with a hyphen. Compound words are words that are joined together without a hyphen. Hyphenated and compound words can be difficult to remember, because sometimes even dictionaries disagree on how these words are spelled. Double-digit numbers like *twenty-two* are always written with a hyphen, and words like *basketball* and *waterfall* are always written as compound words. Disagreements arise most often with more modern phrases. A pad that goes under a computer mouse is spelled *mouse pad* by some people and *mousepad* by other people. If the word remains in use for a long time, one spelling or the other will probably win out.

There are, however, some rules that can help you remember when to hyphenate. You should use a hyphen

➥ when two or more words are combined as a single adjective, such as *one-way street*, *dog-eared page*, or *two-year-old boy*.

➥ with words that describe job titles or family relationships, such as *editor-in-chief*, *mother-in-law*, or *half-brother*.

➥ after the prefixes *ex-*, *self-*, and *all-* (*ex-husband*, *self-employed*, *all-encompassing*), as well as before the suffix *-elect* (*president-elect*, *governor-elect*).

➥ when joining a prefix to a capitalized word, such as *mid-Atlantic* or *un-American*.

➥ with fractions and double-digit numbers that are represented by more than one word, such as *one-half*, *two-thirds*, or *eighty-three*. (Note: this hyphenation rule applies only to the numbers *twenty-one* through *ninety-nine*. For example, *three hundred and forty-three thousand*.)

➥ to combine numbers with nouns, as in *fifty-dollar ticket*, *four-year term*.

➥ to avoid confusion, as when combining two words would create an awkwardly spelled word (*shell-like* instead of *shelllike*).

➥ to form ethnic designations, such as *Chinese-American* or *Indo-European*.

CAUTION!

THE PHRASES *year-old*, *years old*, and *o'clock* are common sources of hyphenated confusion. Remember that words used as a single adjective are hyphenated. So in the phrase *ten-year-old boy*, the words *ten-year-old* form a single adjective. Notice that there isn't a hyphen between *old* and *boy*. This is because *boy* is the noun that the phrase *ten-year-old* is modifying. On the other hand, if you said that the boy was *ten years old*, you would not use any hyphens. In this case, the words *ten* and *years* are not being used as one adjective; the word *ten* is an adjective that modifies *years*, and the word *years* is a modifier that describes *old*.

So far, so good. Here's where it gets tricky. If you want to say your friend is a *ten-year-old*, the words are hyphenated. "But why?" you ask in shock. "This seems to go against all known laws of nature!" The reason is this: In the phrase *ten-year-old*, the noun is implied. It is a unique case in which, for some mysterious reason, over the years, the adjective phrase *ten-year-old* has become accepted as a noun. So to repeat: When the phrase *[number]-year-old* comes before the noun or is used as a noun, it is hyphenated. If the phrase comes after the noun, it is not hyphenated and is often plural: *Ben is five years old*.

The final rule involving time is an easy one. Numbers used with the phrase *o'clock* do not have a hyphen, such as *three o'clock* or *twelve o'clock*. The phrase *o'clock* is a shortened form of "of the clock." It's a strange phrase to have such a prominent place in our daily lives, but at least you know how to spell it now!

PRACTICE LAP

Choose the correct word or phrase to complete each of the following sentences.

21. My (*mother in law/mother-in-law*) lives in Florida.

22. My dog Nachos was (*very-happy/very happy*) to be home.

23. Cindy was proud of her (*Japanese-American/Japanese American*) heritage.

24. Sixteen (*seven-year-olds/seven year olds*) were on the field trip to the museum.

25. The chances of that are highly (*unlikely/un-likely*).

Check your answers at the end of the chapter. How did you do?

CROSSING THE FINISH LINE

In this chapter, we learned that a large percentage of English words come from Latin or Greek. Most words consist of roots, which establish the basic meanings of the words, and prefixes and/or suffixes. When trying to understand words, it can be helpful to divide words into syllables.

Prefixes and suffixes are groups of letters that connect to roots to create words. Prefixes come before the root, and suffixes come after the root. Both suffixes and prefixes enhance or change the meaning of a word. Suffixes also determine which part of speech the word will be. Finally, we learned the rules for hyphenated and compound words.

GAME TIME: NOTABLE QUOTABLE

In the following groups of words, decide which word is spelled correctly. Then take the letter next to that word and enter it into the corresponding blank on page 65. The final answer will spell a famous quote from the philosopher Aristotle.

1.	M vizible	N visable	O visible	P vizable
2.	H exsceed	I exceed	J exseed	K exsede
3.	R recede	S resede	T receed	U reseid
4.	B cownterpart	C countrpart	D cointerpart	E counterpart
5.	R bareable	S bearable	T barable	U bearible
6.	D digestible	E dijestible	F digestable	G digestibel
7.	P pravented	Q previnted	R prevented	S pervented
8.	A tranquil	B trankuil	C tranqwil	D trancuil
9.	H incredable	I incredible	J inkredable	K incridable

10. F ecscusable   G excuesable   H excuzable   I excusable

11. D reeces   E recess   F ricese   G resess

12. R unlikly   S unlikelie   T unlikely   U unliekly

13. O amazement   P amasement   Q amazment   R amazemint

14. A confied   B confid   C confeid   D confide

15. M fashioneable   N fashionible   O fashionabel   P fashionable

16. A ameable   B amieble   C amiable   D amyable

17. B odible   C oddeble   D audable   E audible

18. T reversible   U reversable   V reversabel   W reversibel

19. O invisible   P invicible   Q envisible   R envicible

20. J instinchual   K instinktuel   L instinctual   M instincjual

21. T vizion   U vision   V vishon   W visian

22. D comfterble   E comfertable   F comfortable   G comfortible

23. V repulsive   W ripulsive   X repulsave   Y rapulsave

24. A pripare   B prepare   C prepair   D propair

25. Q credt   R credat   S credet   T credit

26. F rivert   G refert   H revert   I reverte

27. E entroduce   F introduse   G introduce   H entraduce

28. S disable	T disible	U disaible	V desaible
29. I proceed	J proseed	K prosede	L procede
30. D valuble	E valuable	F valable	G valueble
31. M cretable	N cretible	O credible	P credeble
32. K pedle	L pedel	M peddal	N pedal
33. A transmit	B transmitt	C transsmit	D transsmitt
34. R edable	S edible	T edibel	U edibal
35. L resel	M resele	N reselle	O resell
36. M goodnis	N goodness	O goodniss	P goodnes

___ ___ ___ ___ ___ ___ ___ ___ ___   ___ ___   ___ ___ ___
4   14   21   16   8   25   2   35   32   10   28   18   26   11

___ ___ ___ ___   ___ ___ ___ ___ ___ ___ ___ ___ ___   ___ ___ ___
24   30   5   12   15   3   31   23   29   34   9   19   36   22   1   7

___ ___ ___   ___ ___ ___.
13   20   6   33   27   17

CHAPTER 3 WORD LIST

affix (ă′fĭkz)
amazement (ə-māz′mĕnt)
amiable (ā′mē-əbəl)
audible (ô′dĭ-bəl)
base (bās)
bearable (bâr′ə-bəl)

chronic (krŏnˊĭk)

comfortable (kŭmftˊər-bəl)

compound (kŏm-pownd)

confide (kŭnˊfīd)

cooperatively (kō-ŏpˊər-ə-tĭv-lē)

counterpart (kownˊtər-pärt)

credible (krĕdˊĭ-bəl)

credit (krĕdˊĭt)

digestible (dī-jĕstˊə-bəl)

disable (dĭs-āˊbəl)

edible (ĕdˊĭ-bəl)

exceed (ĕkˊsēd)

excusable (ĕk-skyûzˊə-bəl)

fashionable (făˊshən-ə-bəl)

fiction ((fĭkˊshən)

fictional (fĭkˊshən-əl)

goodness (gŏŏdˊnĭs)

hyphenated (hīˊfən-āt-ĭd)

incredible (ĭn-krĕdˊə-bəl)

incredulous (ĭn-krĕdˊyû-ləs)

instinctual (ĭn-stĭnktˊ-yû-əl)

introduce (ĭn-trō-düsˊ)

invisible (ĭn-vĭzˊə-bəl)

nonfiction (nŏnˊfĭk-shən)

omnipotent (ŏm-nĭˊpōˊtĭnt)

omnivore (ŏmˊnĭ-vôr)

omnivorous (ŏmˊnĭˊvôr-əs)

pedal (pĕdˊəl)

predetermined (prē-də-tərˊmĭnd)

prefix (prēˊfĭkz)

prepare (prə-pârˊ)

prevented (prə-vĕntˊĭd)

proceed (prō-sēdˊ)

recede (rə-sēdˊ)

recess (rēˊsĕs)

repulsive (rē-pŭlˊsĭv)

resell (rē´sĕl)

reversible (rē-vərs´ə-bəl)

revert (rē-vərt´)

root (rüt)

suffix (sŭ´fĭkz)

syllables (sĭl´ə-bəlz)

tranquil (trăn´kwĭl)

transmit (trănz-mĭt´)

unable (ŭn-ā´bəl)

unlikely (ŭn-līk´lē)

unremittingly (ŭn-rē-mĭt´ĭng-lē)

valuable (văl´yû-bəl)

visible (vĭz´ĭ-bəl)

vision (vĭzh´ən)

ANSWERS

1. **a. send.** The root *mit* means "send" and the prefix *trans-* means "across." You would *transmit* a message to someone.
2. **c. sell again.** The prefix *re-* means "again."
3. **b. peaceful.** The root word *qui* means "quiet"; therefore, a *tranquil* day would be a peaceful day.
4. **d. determined before.** The prefix *pre-* means "before." Results that were *predetermined* would be determined before.
5. **a. friendly.** The root *am* means "love" and the suffix *-able* means "capable of." Someone who is "capable of love" would be considered friendly.
6. **aud.** The root *aud* means "to hear."
7. **chron.** The root *chron* means "time."
8. **ceed.** The root *ceed* is part of the root family *ced/ceed/cess*, which means "to go, to yield, or to stop."
9. **fid.** The root *fid* means "faith or trust."
10. **ped.** The root *ped* means "foot."
11. **un-, -ly.** The prefix *un-* means "not," and the suffix *-ly* is a common adverb suffix.
12. **intro-.** The prefix *intro-* means "in, into, or within."
13. **re-.** The prefix *re-* means "back or again."

14. **in-, -al.** The prefix *in-* means "not," and the suffix *-al* means "action or process."

15. **-ment.** The suffix *-ment* means "action or process."

16. **pre-.** The prefix *pre-* means "before."

17. **counter-.** The prefix *counter-* means "against."

18. **-ness.** The suffix *-ness* means "state, condition, quality, or degree."

19. **re-, -ive.** The prefix *re-* means "back or again," and the suffix *-ive* means "performing or tending toward."

20. **co-, -at, -ive, -ly.** The prefix *co-* means "with, together, or jointly." The suffix *-at* (or *-ate*) means "to make, to cause to be, or become," the suffix *-ive* means "performing or tending toward," and the suffix-*ly* turns the word into an adverb.

21. **mother-in-law.** *Mother-in-law* is a specific family title, so all the words are hyphenated.

22. **very happy.** *Very* is an adverb that modifies the word *happy*; no hyphen is required.

23. **Japanese-American.** Ethnic designations like *Japanese-American* should be hyphenated.

24. **seven-year-olds.** In the phrase *seven-year-olds*, the noun is implied; in this case, the words should be hyphenated.

25. **unlikely.** *Unlikely* is an adverb with a prefix; no hyphen is required.

Game Time: Notable Quotable Solution

1. O visible
2. I exceed
3. R recede
4. E counterpart
5. S bearable
6. D digestible
7. R prevented
8. A tranquil
9. I incredible
10. I excusable
11. E recess
12. T unlikely
13. O amazement
14. D confide

15. P fashionable
16. C amiable
17. E audible
18. T reversible
19. O invisible
20. L instinctual
21. U vision
22. F comfortable
23. V repulsive
24. B prepare
25. T credit
26. H revert
27. G introduce
28. S disable
29. I proceed
30. E valuable
31. O credible
32. N pedal
33. A transmit
34. S edible
35. O resell
36. N goodness

Quote:

E	D	U	C	A	T	I	O	N		I	S		T	H	E
4	14	21	16	8	25	2	35	32		10	28		18	26	11

B	E	S	T		P	R	O	V	I	S	I	O	N		F	O	R
24	30	5	12		15	3	31	23	29	34	9	19	36		22	1	7

O	L	D		A	G	E	.
13	20	6		33	27	17	

Vowels
The Long and the Short of It All

The five vowels—*a*, *e*, *i*, *o*, and *u*—are very important letters. Almost every syllable of every word in the dictionary contains one of these five letters. Notice I said *almost*. I'm sure you learned a long time ago that there are some words, like *why*, *shy*, and *rhythm*, that use *y* as a vowel. Vowels are so important to pronunciation that we have to draft a consonant to do their job when they can't be found!

A vowel is defined as "a sound that is produced without blocking the passage of air from the throat." You can open your mouth and make all the vowel sounds while keeping your tongue and lips motionless. Try it! By contrast, now try keeping your mouth open and saying a consonant, like *b*, *f*, or *m*. Any luck? I didn't think so! Even trained ventriloquists (vĕn-trĭl'ō-kwĭsts: entertainers who project their voices so that the sound appears to come from elsewhere, usually a dummy or puppet) can't get around the basic science of how we make sounds. With practice, a ventriloquist can train herself to move her lips very little when speaking, but she can never make these sounds come entirely from her throat.

FUEL FOR THOUGHT

IT'S NOT NECESSARY that an English word contain an *a, e, i, o,* or *u,* but it *is* important that every word have at least the *sound* of one of these letters. In the words in which *y* is used as a vowel, the *y* makes a long ī sound (m**y**) or a short i sound (h**y**mn).

There is, as always, a tiny handful of exceptions. Take *sh,* for instance. You probably know exactly what is meant when you read the letters *sh.* We've all heard our teachers and parents use this noise to quiet us down. Although it is consistently written the same way, *sh* belongs to that strange class of words known as interjections. Interjections are words used to express emotions; they are not grammatically related to the other parts of a sentence. *Psst,* the sound you might make if you had to tell someone a secret, is another interjection that has no vowels. Although interjections are technically words, they can disobey the rules because they represent sounds, not parts of speech.

Trivia fans in the reading audience should note that there are two other words in some dictionaries that have no vowels—*cwm* (pronounced [küm]: a glacial basin without walls) and *crwth* (pronounced [krüth]: a musical instrument). These words originally came from Welsh, where *w* sometimes makes a vowel sound. Chances are very strong that you will never have any reason to use either of these words in conversation, but they can save your life in a game of Scrabble!

PRACTICE LAP

Choose the correct spelling of each of the following words.

1. pride/pryde

2. shi/shy

3. linx/lynx

4. wicker/wycker

5. tried/tryed

6. dynamic/dinamic

7. mith/myth

8. cript/crypt

9. sigh/sygh

10. whine/whyne

Check your answers at the end of the chapter. How did you do?

VOWEL SOUNDS

There are two main types of vowels: short and long. The letter *a* is pronounced one way in the word *cat* and another way in the word *late*. The *a* in *cat* is considered a short vowel, while the *a* in *late* is considered a long vowel. Technically, short vowels are sounded in the throat for a shorter amount of time than long vowels. It might be easier to remember that long vowels are vowels that seem to say their own names. Examples of long vowels are *a* as in *game* and *tale*, *e* as in *feed* or *scene*, *i* as in *flight* or *pine*, *o* as in *bone* or *toe*, and *u* as in *compute* or *unicorn*. Short vowels, on the other hand, include the sound *a* as in *cat* or *acid*, *e* as in *bet* or *felt*, *i* as in *wig* or *bit*, *o* as in *hog* or *monster*, and *u* as in *rug* or *tumble*.

 CAUTION!

THERE IS a third type of vowel sound that is neither short nor long, and it has a very strange name: the **schwa** (*shwä*). The schwa is what a vowel sounds like when it is unstressed in an unstressed syllable. This is represented in the pronunciation charts with the strange

upside-down *e* that looks like this: ə. The ə is found in words like
***a**bout*, ***a**dult*, *th**e**, penc**i**l, bish**o**p*, and *s**u**pply*. Because all vowels
can make the ə sound, it is actually the most common vowel sound
in the English language.

Schwa vowels often lead to spelling errors, because every letter
can make this same sound. For instance, nothing can be heard in
the pronunciation of the word *calendar* to indicate that it should end
in *-ar*; the exact same sound can be heard, spelled differently, in the
words *butter, fir, major*, and *burr*. In some cases, an understanding
of suffixes can help you determine spelling of schwa vowels but not
always. Be on the lookout for words like *calendar* that might just
need to be memorized.

The way to determine whether a vowel will be long or short is to look at
the consonants surrounding it. Generally, when a single vowel is found by
itself in a short word or syllable (three or four letters), it will make the short
sound. You can go through the alphabet letter by letter and come up with
numerous examples: *bad, bed, big, bog, bud*, and so on.

There are two instances in which vowels are long: in vowel + consonant
+ silent *e* combinations, such as *bake, bike*, and *poke*, and when the vowel
appears at the end of a single-syllable word, as in *be, no*, and *go*.

"Now hold on there, buddy," you might say to me. "Just off the top of
my head, I can think of plenty of words in which the vowels don't make
either of these sounds. What about *star*, for instance? That *a* sounds
nothing like the *a* in *apple* or the *a* in *game*! What about *fierce*, or *born*, or
pure?"

That is a great question, and I am happy to report that I have an answer.
Certain combinations of vowels and consonants can change the sound of
the vowel. The *a* sound in *star*, for instance, is created by the combination
of *a* and *r*. This same combination can be found in many other words such
as *car, bar, harm*, and *yard*. The letter *r* is a powerful force in pronunciation,
and vowels that are coupled with this letter have their own special category
called **r-controlled vowels.**

R-Controlled Vowels

Vowels that are followed by the letter *r* are called r-controlled vowels. The table below lists the different r-controlled vowel sounds.

(är)   y**ar**d
(âr)   c**are**
(îr)   p**ier**
(ôr)   t**or**n
(ər)   calend**ar**
(yûr)   c**ure**

CAUTION!

THE SILENT *e* may not make any noise, but it sure has an awful lot of power. It can turn a *star* into a *stare* and a *cur* into a *cure*. You'll notice in these cases that the vowel is almost pronounced as if it were long. The result of the struggle between the *r* sound and the silent *e* is a new vowel sound that is almost similar to a long vowel but not quite.

PRACTICE LAP

Fill in the correct r-controlled vowel combinations in the following words.

11. second __ __ y

12. sut __ __ e

13. transf __ __ m

14. sh __ __ ehold __ __

15. ph __ __ macy

Check your answers at the end of the chapter. How did you do?

Diphthongs

Diphthongs (dĭf'thôngz or dĭp'thôngz) are complex vowel sounds that are created when two vowel sounds are blended together. For example, say the *ow* sound in the word *cow* very slowly. Can you hear how the vowel starts out with an *ahhh* sound and slides into an *ooo* sound?

That is what a diphthong sounds like. The most common diphthongs are listed in the following chart.

au	caution
aw	jaw
oi	coin
oy	joy
ou	mouse
ow	cow

PRACTICE LAP

Complete the following words with the proper diphthong.

16. f __ __ ndation

17. b __ __ sterous

18. d __ __ ghter

19. unempl __ __ ed

20. __ __ thority

Vowel + Vowel Combinations

A popular mnemonic says, "When two vowels go walking, the first does the talking." This means that in combinations of multiple vowels, the first vowel will usually be pronounced with a long vowel sound, while the second vowel will remain silent. The following table lists common vowel + vowel combinations that follow this rule.

ai (ā)	brain
ee/ea/ei (ē)	peek
ie (ī)	die
oa/oe (ō)	toast
ue/ui (ū)	cue

Of course, in English pronunciation, no rule ever applies to every single word. The following is a list of the most common exceptions to the "when two vowels go walking" rule.

ea (ĕ)	head
ei (ā)	vein
ei (ī)	heist
ie (ē)	brief
oo (ŏŏ)	foot
oo (ü)	boot
ou (ü)	you
ou (ŭ)	nervous

Please note that in all of the preceding examples, the two vowels combine within a single syllable. If the vowels are split between two syllables, each vowel will retain its individual pronunciation. Compare, for example, the differences between the *ea* combination in the words *plea* and *idea*. *Plea* is a single syllable word, and the *ea* combination follows the "when vowels go walking" rule. *Idea*, on the other hand, is a two-syllable word, so this rule is not followed. Another situation in which this spelling occurs is as a result of affix + root combinations. Examples of this include words like *trial* (trī'əl), *preamp* (prē'ămp), and *simian* (sĭm'ē-ən).

PRACTICE LAP

Choose the correctly spelled italicized word in each of the following sentences.

21. The magician (*instantaneously/instantaneusly*) disappeared.

22. Although I did not want to appear (*boastful/bosteful*), I was proud to have scored the highest grade on the test.

23. The tent (*sheilded/shielded*) us from the punishing rain.

24. Allan's pet parrot sat contentedly on her (*roust/roost*).

25. Mrs. Worthington asked us to set up our (*easels/eesals*) and begin painting.

Check your answers at the end of the chapter. How did you do?

Vowel + Consonant Combinations

There are a number of common vowel + consonant combinations that you can learn to help in your spelling. The most common of these combinations are listed here.

ay (ā)	Friday
wa/ua (wô)	walk
wa/ua (wă)	swam
al/all/oll (ôl)	altar
ew (ü)	slew
ey (ē)	monkey
ey/ye (ī)	geyser
ol/oll (ōl)	fold
ost (ôst)	cost
ost (ōst)	most
ow (ōw)	bowl
qu (kw)	queen

PRACTICE LAP

Choose the correctly spelled italicized word in each of the following sentences.

26. I believe the quality of food at a meal is more important than the (*kwantity/quantity*).

27. A single hair (*follicle/fallicle*) was perched on the edge of the sink.

28. I found the events in the movie to be absolutely (*preposterous/ prepasterous*).

29. After a few days, fruit will begin to (*decai/decay*).

30. Muhammad Ali was once the (*undisputed/undispewted*) world heavy-weight champion.

Check your answers at the end of the chapter. How did you do?

CROSSING THE FINISH LINE

In this chapter we studied vowels and vowel combinations. A vowel is a sound that is produced without blocking the passage of air from the throat. The vowels are *a, e, i, o, u,* and sometimes *y.* With the exception of a handful of interjections, these letters can be found in every word of the English language.

There are two main types of vowels, short vowels and long vowels. Long vowels are vowels that seem to say their own names, like the *a* in *bake* or the *i* in *bike.* All vowels can also make another sound called the schwa sound. When a vowel is found by itself in a short word or syllable, it will usually make a short sound. Long vowels are generally found in vowel + consonant + silent *e* combinations, or at the end of a single-syllable word.

Vowel + consonant and vowel + vowel combinations sometimes affect the way individual vowels are pronounced. R-controlled vowels are vowels that are followed by the letter *r.* Diphthongs are vowel combinations in which two vowel sounds are blended together.

In a large number of cases, when two vowels are found next to each other, the first vowel will be pronounced and the second vowel will be silent. This rule can be remembered by the mnemonic "When two vowels go walking, the first does the talking." We also saw a selection of vowel + consonant combinations that result in unique pronunciations, such as *wa*, *all*, and *ost*.

GAME TIME: SPELLING SCRAMBLE

Each of the following contains a scrambled word from the Chapter 4 word list with one extra letter. The number of letters in the final word is written in the parentheses next to each scrambled word. Write the unscrambled word in the blanks. When you're done, you will have one letter left over. Enter these letters in order in the puzzle to find a quote from the comedian Stephen Wright. (If you get stuck, there are clues following the scrambled word list.)

1. eopyprrseotus (12) __ __ __ __ __ __ __ __ __ __ __ __

2. oedyac (5) __ __ __ __ __

3. geutdhrua (8) __ __ __ __ __ __ __ __

4. ricpde (5) __ __ __ __ __

5. yerancdsao (9) __ __ __ __ __ __ __ __ __

6. eitndr (5) __ __ __ __ __

7. jentorectinit (12) __ __ __ __ __ __ __ __ __ __ __ __

8. lllefchio (8) __ __ __ __ __ __ __ __

9. enrldcaaa (8) __ __ __ __ __ __ __ __

10. sotrov (5) __ __ __ __ __

11. tereusu (6) __ __ __ __ __ __

12. eoumednpley (10) __ __ __ __ __ __ __ __ __ __

13. unvaqtyit (8) __ __ __ __ __ __ __ __

14. mehyt (4) — — — —

15. seaelrs (6) — — — — — —

16. lafstyuob (8) — — — — — — — —

17. mcdnitya (7) — — — — — — —

18. udhonnoatfi (10) — — — — — — — — — —

19. thihmyr (6) — — — — — —

20. nesliedhd (8) — — — — — — — —

21. rnftamgosr (9) — — — — — — — — —

22. rwymaacph (8) — — — — — — — —

23. nwehhi (5) — — — — —

24. yetlsitousnnanae (15) — — — — — — — — — — — — — — —

25. htiatorruy (9) — — — — — — — — —

26. sroseibetou (10) — — — — — — — — — —

27. pwcytr (5) — — — — —

28. noylx (4) — — — —

29. sghui (4) — — — —

30. sduiledtpnu (10) — — — — — — — — — —

31. dhyw (3) — — —

32. kicweyr (6)   _ _ _ _ _ _

33. oyhs (3)   _ _ _

34. oncsatnuno (9)   _ _ _ _ _ _ _ _ _

35. hdinppogth (9)   _ _ _ _ _ _ _ _ _

36. wuveosl (6)   _ _ _ _ _ _

37. hhtearoelsrd (11)   _ _ _ _ _ _ _ _ _ _ _

38. tcrihw (5)   _ _ _ _ _

39. osvntirtetuliq (13)   _ _ _ _ _ _ _ _ _ _ _ _ _

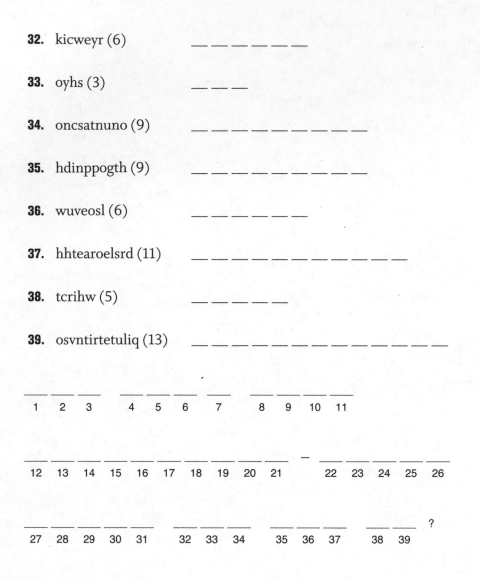

_ _ _ _ _ _ _ _ _ _ _
1 2 3   4 5 6 7   8 9 10 11

_ _ _ _ _ _ _ _ _ _ _ _ _ _ _ _
12 13 14 15 16 17 18 19 20 21   22 23 24 25 26

_ _ _ _ _ _ _ _ _ _ _ _ _ ?
27 28 29 30 31   32 33 34   35 36 37   38 39

Spelling Scramble Clues

1. First letter: p   Last letter: s

2. First letter: d   Last letter: y

3. First letter: d   Last letter: r

4. First letter: p   Last letter: e

5. First letter: s   Last letter: y

6. First letter: t   Last letter: d

7. First letter: i   Last letter: n

8. First letter: f   Last letter: e

9. First letter: c   Last letter: r

10. First letter: r   Last letter: t

11. First letter: s   Last letter: e

12. First letter: u   Last letter: d

13. First letter: q   Last letter: y

14. First letter: m   Last letter: h

15. First letter: e   Last letter: s

16. First letter: b   Last letter: l

17. First letter: d   Last letter: c

18. First letter: f   Last letter: n

19. First letter: r   Last letter: m

20. First letter: s   Last letter: d

21. First letter: t   Last letter: m

22. First letter: p   Last letter: y

23. First letter: w   Last letter: e

24. First letter: i   Last letter: y

25. First letter: a   Last letter: y

26. First letter: b   Last letter: s

27. First letter: c   Last letter: t

28. First letter: l   Last letter: x

29. First letter: s   Last letter: h

30. First letter: u   Last letter: d

31. First letter: w   Last letter: y

32. First letter: w   Last letter: r

33. First letter: s   Last letter: y

34. First letter: c   Last letter: t

35. First letter: d   Last letter: g

36. First letter: v   Last letter: s

37. First letter: s   Last letter: r

38. First letter: c   Last letter: h

39. First letter: v   Last letter: t

CHAPTER 4 WORD LIST

authority (ô-thōr'-ĭ-tē)
boastful (bōst'fəl)
boisterous (boist'ər-əs)
calendar (kăl'ən-dər)

consonant (kŏn'sən-ənt)

crwth (krüth)

crypt (krĭpt)

cwm (küm)

daughter (dôt'ər)

decay (dē-kā')

diphthong (dĭf'thông or dĭp'thông)

dynamic (dī-năm'ĭk)

easels (ē'zəlz)

follicle (fŏl'ĭ-kəl)

foundation (fownd-ā'shŭn)

instantaneously (ĭn-stent-ān'ē-əs-lē)

interjection (ĭn-tər-jĕk'shŭn)

lynx (lĭnkz)

myth (mĭth)

pharmacy (fârm'ə-sē)

preposterous (prə-pŏst'ər-əs)

pride (prīd)

quantity (kwŏn'tĭ-tē)

rhythm (rĭthm)

roost (rüst)

schwa (shwä)

secondary (sĕk'ənd-ār-ē)

shareholder (shār'hōld-ər)

shielded (shēld'əd)

shy (shī)

sigh (sī)

suture (sü'chər)

transform (trăns'fôrm)

tried (trīd)

undisputed (ŭn-dĭs-pyû'təd)

unemployed (ŭn-ĕm-ploid')

ventriloquist (vĕn-trĭl'ō-kwĭst)

vowels (vow'əlz)

whine (wīn)

why (wī)

wicker (wĭk'ər)

ANSWERS

1. **pride.** When a silent *e* is found at the end of a word, the vowel will have a long sound. The silent *e* is discussed later in this chapter.

2. **shy.** The only words in which the letter *i* appears at the end are words that have been borrowed from other languages, such as *confetti* and *spaghetti*. Words from foreign languages are covered in Chapter 10.

3. **lynx.** A *lynx* is a type of wildcat. Animal names are often taken from different languages and do not follow any rules; many of these spellings simply have to be memorized.

4. **wicker.** The letter *y* is never followed by the consonant combination *ck*. You will learn more about consonant combinations in Chapter 5.

5. **tried.** Although the based word of *tried* is *try*, the *y* becomes an *i* when the past form *-ed* is added. Endings are discussed in greater detail in Chapter 6.

6. **dynamic.** *Dynamic* comes from the Greek root *dynamis*, meaning "power." Other words that share this root include *dynasty*, *dynamite*, and *dynamo*.

7. **myth.** *Myth* is an ancient word that has remained relatively unchanged from its Latin root.

8. **crypt.** Like *myth*, *crypt* is an ancient word that remains relatively unchanged from its Latin root.

9. **sigh.** *I* + silent *gh* generally produces a long *i* sound, as in *high*, *night*, and *light*. Read more about the silent *gh* combination in Chapter 5.

10. **whine.** This is another example of the common long *i* + silent *e* combination.

11. **secondary.** The ending *-ary* is a common noun suffix meaning "belonging or connected to."

12. **suture.** *Suture* is a surgical term meaning "to join together by stitching." Stitches are sutures. The r-controlled vowel is pronounced (ûr), as in *pure* and *sure*.

13. **transform.** This word combines the Latin root *form* with the prefix *trans-*, meaning "across."

14. **shareholder.** There are two r-controlled vowels in this word; *ar* pronounced (ãr), and *er* pronounced (ər). In the first r-controlled vowel, the pronunciation is determined by the silent *e*. The second r-controlled vowel is a common schwa combination.

15. pharmacy. *Pharmacy* comes from the Greek root *pharma*, meaning "drug." Other words that share this root are *pharmacist* and *pharmaceutical*.

16. foundation

17. boisterous

18. daughter

19. unemployed

20. authority

21. **instantaneously.** The common adjective ending *-ous* means "full of, having the qualities of, or relating to." This suffix does not follow the "when two vowels go walking" rule, so be sure to remember that it is pronounced (ŭs).

22. **boastful.** The vowel combination *oa* follows the "when two vowels go walking" rule.

23. **shielded.** The mnemonic "i before e, except after c" pertains in this situation.

24. **roost.** Although *roust* is a word, a *roost* is something a parrot would sit on. In this case, *roost* is pronounced (rŏŏst).

25. **easels.** The word *easels* has the same root as *easy.* The "when two vowels go walking, the first does the talking" rule works in this case.

26. **quantity.** The (kw) sound is almost always made by the *qu* vowel + consonant combination.

27. **follicle.** The vowel + consonant combination *oll* is pronounced (ôl) in this case, as in the words *doll* and *holly.*

28. **preposterous.** In this case, you might look at your knowledge of suffixes and prefixes and assume that the root of the word *preposterous* was pronounced similarly to the word *post.* In this case, however, the *ost* sound is pronounced (ôst), as in *cost.*

29. **decay.** As mentioned earlier, it is rare to find an English word that ends with an *i. Decay* is the correct spelling of this word.

30. **undisputed.** In this case, you may have removed the suffixes and prefixes and assumed that the root of this word was *put.* The base word in this case, however, is *dispute.* The vowel + consonant + silent *e* rule tells you how to spell this word.

Game Time: Spelling Scramble Solution

1. preposterous
2. decay
3. daughter
4. pride
5. secondary
6. tried
7. interjection
8. follicle
9. calendar
10. roost
11. suture
12. unemployed
13. quantity
14. myth
15. easels
16. boastful
17. dynamic
18. foundation
19. rhythm
20. shielded
21. transform
22. pharmacy
23. whine
24. instantaneously
25. authority
26. boisterous
27. crypt
28. lynx
29. sigh
30. undisputed
31. why
32. wicker
33. shy
34. consonant
35. diphthong
36. vowels

37. shareholder

38. crwth

39. ventriloquist

Quote:

Y O U   C A N ' T   H A V E
‾‾ ‾‾ ‾‾   ‾‾ ‾‾ ‾‾ ‾‾   ‾‾ ‾‾ ‾‾ ‾‾
1 2 3   4 5 6 7   8 9 10 11

E V E R Y T H I N G — W H E R E
‾‾ ‾‾ ‾‾ ‾‾ ‾‾ ‾‾ ‾‾ ‾‾ ‾‾ ‾‾   ‾‾ ‾‾ ‾‾ ‾‾ ‾‾
12 13 14 15 16 17 18 19 20 21   22 23 24 25 26

W O U L D   Y O U   P U T   I T   ?
‾‾ ‾‾ ‾‾ ‾‾ ‾‾   ‾‾ ‾‾ ‾‾   ‾‾ ‾‾ ‾‾   ‾‾ ‾‾
27 28 29 30 31   32 33 34   35 36 37   38 39

The Consistent Consonant

Ah, consonants—the old, reliable workhorses of pronunciation. Unlike those pesky vowels, which can make all kinds of different sounds, the 21 consonants are nice and dependable. The *b* in *boy* is the same as the *b*s in *bubble*, which are the same as the *b*s in *babbling brook*. Six consonants can make two or three different sounds—*c*, *g*, *q*, *s*, *x*, and *y*—but for the most part, it is clear which pronunciation is called for in a given word.

Consonants are created by blocking the flow of air from the throat using the lips or tongue. There are six different mouth positions used to produce the consonants, which are described in the following table.

Shape Name	Shape Description	Letters Formed Using this Shape
alveolar (ăl-vē-ō′lər)	tip of the tongue near the back of the upper teeth	t, d, j, n
bilabial (bī-lāb′ē-əl)	lips press together and pull apart	b, m, p, w
labiodental (lāb′ē-ō-děnt-əl)	lower lip presses against the upper teeth	f, v

linguadental (lǐng´gwə-děnt-əl)	middle of the tongue presses near the back of the upper teeth	s, z
palatal (pāl´ə-təl)	front of the tongue touches the hard palate	y
velar (vē´lər)	back of the tongue touches the upper palate	g, k, q

If you're reading this, of course, you already know the sounds that the different letters make, but here's a quick refresher:

b	boy		p	paid
c	place, case		r	record, super
d	dog		s	sound, trees
f	effort		t	item
g	agent, agree		v	violin
h	how		w	welcome
j	junk		x	ax, xylophone, exist
l	aloud, camel		y	you, myth, dye, candy
m	money		z	zip
n	nail, sudden			

ODD CONSONANTS OUT

Of the 21 consonants, c, q, and x are the only ones that do not make their own unique sounds. C can make two different sounds, both of which are also made by other letters. It either sounds like an s, as in the word dice, or a k, as in the word cry. In some words, like accent and succinct, it makes both sounds.

The letter q rarely appears without its friend u. There are a few words in the dictionary in which the word q appears without u, but these are mainly words that have been borrowed from other languages, such as cinq (meaning five), or place names, like Qatar (a country in the Middle East). The English q + u combination can either be pronounced kw, as in queen, or k, as in unique.

X can represent three different sounds. When it appears at the beginning of a word (which is not very often), it usually sounds like a *z*, as in *xylophone* or *Xerox*. When it follows the letter *e* at the beginning of a word it can sometimes make a *gs* sound, as in *exact* or *exert*. In all other cases, *x* will make a *ks* sound, as in *box*, *taxi*, or *extinct*.

INSIDE TRACK

Both *c* and *g* can make two different sounds, which are classified as either *soft* or *hard*. The soft *c* is pronounced like an *s*, and the hard *c* is pronounced with a *k* sound. The soft *g* is pronounced with a *j* sound, while the hard *g* is pronounced with a *guh* sound. There are two rules to follow when trying to determine whether *c* or *g* will be soft or hard.

1. **When the letter *c* or *g* is followed by an *e*, *i*, or *y*, it will almost always be soft.** The words *cent*, *decide*, and *cymbal* all have soft *c* sounds, while the words *gel*, *giant*, and *gym* all have a soft *g* sound,
2. **When the letter *c* or *g* is followed by *a*, *o*, or *u*, it will almost always be hard.** The words *care*, *cotton*, and *crust* all have hard *c* sounds, while the words *game*, *got*, and *guppy* all have a hard *g* sound.

PRACTICE LAP

Choose the correctly spelled italicized word in each of the following sentences.

1. My grandfather works (*ceaselessly/seacelessly*) even though he's over 80 years old.

2. Mr. Baron is a high-ranking (*egsecutive/executive*) at the ad agency.

3. Children are considered (*juveniles/guveniles*) until they turn 18.

4. We were thinking about seeing a movie today, but it's not really (*feasible/ feezible*) with our packed schedule.

5. I need an (*access/axess*) code to get into my e-mail (*akount/account*).

Check your answers at the end of the chapter. How did you do?

CONSONANT COMBINATIONS

Digraphs and Trigraphs

Although you may not know it, you've already studied digraphs in this book. The diphthongs we studied in Chapter 4 were all examples of **digraphs** (dī′grăfs): two-letter combinations that make a single sound. **Trigraphs** (trī′grăfs) are three-letter combinations that make a single sound. The most common digraphs and trigraphs can be found in the table below.

bt	(bt)	de**bt**	ph	(f)	**ph**one
ch	(ch)	whi**ch**	qu	(kw)	**qu**iet
ck	(k)	fli**ck**	qu	(k)	cli**qu**e
ff	(f)	flu**ff**	sh	(sh)	**sh**ift
gh	(g)	**gh**ost	ss	(s)	cla**ss**
gh	(f)	cou**gh**	th	(th)	**th**imble
gn	(n)	**gn**ome	wh	(h)	**wh**o
kn	(n)	**kn**ot	wr	(r)	**wr**en
ll	(l)	ca**ll**	zz	(z)	fu**zz**
mb	(m)	thu**mb**	dge	(j)	ple**dge**
ng	(ng)	thi**ng**	tch	(ch)	ca**tch**
nk	(nk)	si**nk**			

As you'll notice, most of the digraphs are pronounced as a single letter. For this reason, they can often cause spelling errors. Digraphs like *sh* and *th* are easy to remember, because there are no other letter combinations that produce those sounds. But a strange combination like *mb* can be hard to recall, since the *b* is silent.

The best way to use your knowledge of digraphs and trigraphs is to memorize the 23 letter combinations listed here. As you learn new words that include these digraphs, make a note of them. If you're feeling particularly ambitious, you might even keep a journal of your new words. It is easier to remember how words are spelled when you can see patterns between many words than when you think of each word as completely unique.

PRACTICE LAP

In the following, fill in the missing letters with the correct digraph or trigraph.

6. The giant __ __ ashed his teeth impatiently as he waited for his dinner.

7. In Social Studies class, we sometimes write criti __ __ es of newspaper articles.

8. Every mountain will eventually succu __ __ to the power of the sea.

9. Mr. Stephens is particularly __ __ owle __ __ __ able about nineteenth-century poetry.

10. The guards fla __ __ ed the palace doors.

Check your answers at the end of the chapter. How did you do?

CAUTION!

CONSONANT COMBINATIONS ARE only considered digraphs when they produce a single sound. You can find digraph + letter combinations in other words, but unless they are working together to create a single sound, their placement is purely coincidental. For example, the consonant combination *gh* can be found in the word *foghorn*, but only because this is a compound word composed of the words *fog* and *horn*. Likewise, be careful to draw a distinction between the digraph *ng* as part of words like *king* and *flung*, and the verb ending *-ing* found in words like *jumping* and *thinking*.

Consonant Blends

Consonant combinations in which the letters keep their original sounds are called **consonant blends.** The most common consonant blends are listed in the following tables.

Two-Letter Blends

bl	(bl)	**bl**end	pr	(pr)	**pr**oud
br	(br)	**br**eak	sk	(sk)	**sk**etch
cl	(kl)	**cl**ue	sl	(sl)	**sl**ow
cr	(kr)	in**cr**ease	sm	(sm)	**sm**art
dr	(dr)	**dr**ift	sn	(sn)	**sn**ack
fl	(fl)	**fl**ower	sp	(sp)	**sp**oil
fr	(fr)	**fr**iend	st	(st)	**st**amp
gl	(gl)	**gl**ass	sw	(sw)	**sw**ing
gr	(gr)	**gr**ain	tr	(tr)	**tr**ouble
nd	(nd)	seco**nd**	tw	(tw)	**tw**ist
pl	(pl)	**pl**ace			

Three-Letter Blends

chr	(kr)	**chr**ome	spr	(spr)	**spr**ing
scr	(skr)	**scr**atch	squ	(skw)	**squ**are
shr	(shr)	**shr**ink	str	(str)	**str**aight
spl	(spl)	**spl**ash	thr	(thr)	**thr**ow

You'll notice that a large number of the two- and three-letter blends previously mentioned start with the letter *s*. *S* is a very easy letter to blend, because it slides together nicely with many consonants. By contrast, think of the letter *l*, which does not play nicely when placed at the beginning of words. There are many words that start with *sk* or *sn*, but can you imagine how you would pronounce a word that started with *lk* or *ln*?

PRACTICE LAP

Each of the following sentences is followed by a selection of consonant blends. Choose which consonant blend belongs in each blank space.

11. My teacher gave me the ta___ of re___acing the chips in the hamster's cage and di___osing of his uneaten food. (pl, sk, sp)

12. ___oughout history, the leaders who have shown re___ect for their people have consi___ently been the most beloved. (sp, st, thr)

13. Our host was ex___emely ___acious when I accidentally ___oke her serving ___atter. (br, gr, pl, tr)

14. A ___eme___ous noise arose ___om the ___owd when the race cars ___ arted their engines. (cr, fr, nd, st, tr)

15. As I watched the nature film, I was en___alled by the de___uctive power of the ___ashing waves. (spl, thr, str)

Check your answers at the end of the chapter. How did you do?

KEEP IT QUIET: SILENT LETTERS

Adding a great amount of confusion to spelling is the fact that many consonants can be silent. We've already seen examples of silent letters in digraphs; the letter *b* in the digraph *mb*, or the letter *w* in the diagraph *wr*. Not all of the silent consonants have consistent rules, however. Some of these letters have dropped out of pronunciation after years of usage. The compound word *cupboard* was probably originally pronounced just like it looks (*kŭp'bōrd*), but over the years, it has come to be pronounced with a silent *p* (*kŭb'ərd*). There aren't really any rules to help you with words like these; they just need to be memorized.

   The following is a table of silent-letters combinations that have not been covered already.

p	cupboard, debt, doubt	s	island, aisle
d	handsome, Wednesday	t	castle, mortgage

h	rhyme, honor	ch	yacht
l	calf, calm, would	gh	**high,** although, neighbor
p	psychiatrist, raspberry		

INSIDE TRACK

OF ALL THE common letter combinations, none are more annoying to the budding spelling bee champion than *gh*. Sometimes it's pronounced like an *f* (as in *cough* and *laugh*), sometimes it's pronounced like a *g* (as in *spaghetti* and *ghoul*). Still other times, it isn't pronounced at all. It's often found after the vowel combination *ou*, which can be pronounced (âw) as in *cough*, (ŭ) as in *enough*, (ō) as in *although* (ŏŏ), as in *through*, or (ow) as in *bough*. There are a few rules that can help you remember how to pronounce the *gh*, but not enough to explain every case:

1. **When *ough* or *augh* is followed by a *t*, it almost always represents the (âw) sound.** Examples: *thought, bought, fought, caught, daughter, naughty*
2. **When *gh* is found at the beginning of a word or followed immediately by a vowel, it is always pronounced as a hard *g*.** Examples: *ghoul, ghastly, ghetto, spaghetti*

PRACTICE LAP

Choose the correct spelling of the italicized word in each of the following sentences.

16. I will always be (*indebted/indetted*) to Martin for helping me when I was sick.

17. The dog was (*riled/risled*) up and running around.

18. Sheila took her first airplane (*flite/flight*) this year.

19. Getting to school on time is always such a (*hassle/hastle*).

20. Mozambique has been experiencing a terrible (*drout/drought*) this year.

Check your answers at the end of the chapter. How did you do?

DOUBLE CONSONANTS

In Chapter 6, you'll learn the rules for doubling consonants when adding verb endings like *-ing* or *-ed*. There are a number of other words in the English language with double consonants, however. Some of these words are created by the combination of prefixes and suffixes; for example, the word *overreach* has a double r because of the combination of the prefix *over* and the base word *reach*. Certain endings, such as *-y* and *-le* are commonly attached to words with double consonants—*funny*, *lobby*, and *happy*, for instance, or *apple*, *riddle*, and *rattle*. The only rule to remember with double consonants is that they are almost always pronounced as a single letter.

CROSSING THE FINISH LINE

In this chapter, we learned that consonants are created by blocking the flow of air from the throat using the lips or tongue. Except for the letters *c, g, q, s, x,* and *y,* each consonant makes only one, consistent sound. *C, g, q,* and *s* make two different sounds, while *x* can make three different sounds and *y* can make four different sounds. The letter *q* is almost always followed by the letter *u.* The letters *c* and *g* can be hard or soft. If these letters are followed by an *e, i,* or *y,* they will almost always be soft; if they're followed by an *a, o,* or *u,* they will almost always be hard.

Digraphs are two-letter combinations that make a single sound, while trigraphs are three-letter combinations that make a single sound. Consonant blends are consonant combinations in which the letters keep their original sounds. A small number of consonants can be silent in certain situations; although these consonants can sometimes be remembered as digraphs, there are a few situations in which no rules will apply. Double consonants occur frequently and should be pronounced as a single consonant sound.

GAME TIME: SPELLING JUMBLE

The following boxes feature jumbled-up words from the Chapter 5 word list. Write the unscrambled words in the empty boxes. Then unscramble the circled letters to find the answer to each riddle.

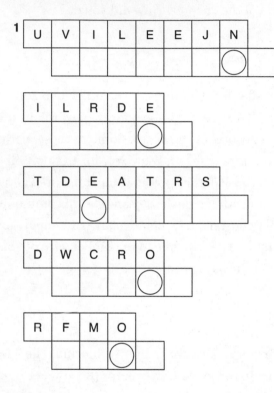

What gets wet the more it dries?

A

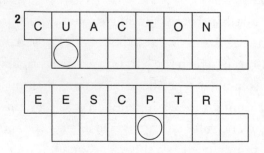

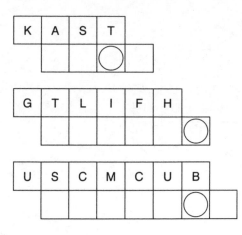

K	A	S	T

G	T	L	I	F	H

U	S	C	M	C	U	B

What goes all around the world but stays in a corner?

A ◯◯◯◯◯

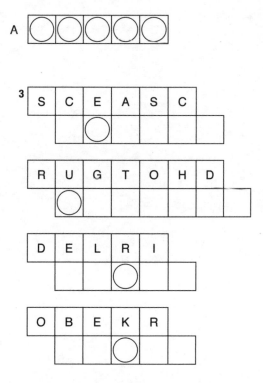

3	S	C	E	A	S	C

R	U	G	T	O	H	D

D	E	L	R	I

O	B	E	K	R

What can you catch but not throw?

A ◯◯◯◯

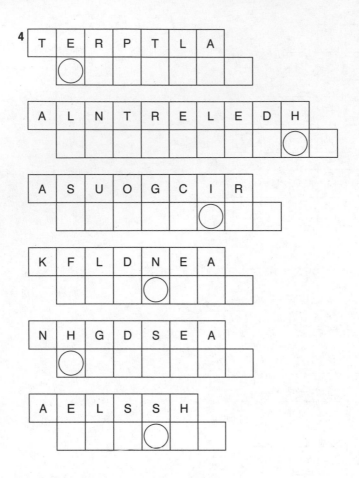

4 T E R P T L A

A L N T R E L E D H

A S U O G C I R

K F L D N E A

N H G D S E A

A E L S S H

What is filled with holes but still holds water?

A

CHAPTER 5 WORD LIST

access (ăk′sĕs)

account (ə-kownt′)

alveolar (ăl-vē-ō′lər)

bilabial (bī-lāb′ē-əl)

broke (brōk)

ceaselessly (sēs′lĕs-lē)

consistently (kŭn-sĭst′ənt-lē)

consonant blends (kŏn′sən-ənt blĕndz)

critiques (crĭ-tēks′)

crowd (krowd)

destructive (də-strŭkt-ĭv)

digraph (dī′grăf)

disposing (dĭs-pōz′ĭng)

drought (drowt)

enthralled (ĕn-thrôld′)

executive (ĕg-zĕk′yû-tĭv)

extremely (eks-trēm′lē)

feasible (fēz′ə-bəl)

flanked (flănkd)

flight (flīt)

from (frŭm)

gnashed (năshd)

gracious (grā′shəs)

hassle (hă′səl)

indebted (ĭn-dĕt′əd)

juvenile (jü′vən-īl)

knowledgeable (nŏl′əj-ə-bəl)

labiodental (lāb′ē-ō-dĕnt-əl)

linguadental (lĭng′gwə-dĕnt-əl)

palatal (pāl′ə-təl)

platter (plăt′ər)

replacing (rē-plās′ĭng)

respect (rē-spĕkt′)

riled (rīld)

splashing (splăsh′ĭng)

started (stârt-əd)

succumb (sŭ-kŭm′)

task (tăsk)

throughout (thrü-owt′)

tremendous (trə-mĕnd′əs)

trigraph (trī′grăf)

velar (vē′lər)

ANSWERS

1. **ceaselessly**. With words that have several *s* sounds; it can be difficult to remember which *s* sound is spelled with *c* and which is spelled with an *s*. In this case, you know that *-less* and *-ly* are suffixes, so any confusion would come with the spelling of the word *cease*. *Cease* is related to the *ced/cede/cess* root. With this knowledge, you can guess that *cease* is probably spelled with the *c* first and the *s* second.

2. **executive**. Although *executive* is pronounced as though the *x* were a *gs*, you should remember that *ex-* is a common prefix. There are no words in the English language that begin with the letters *egs*.

3. **juveniles**. A *g* followed by the letter *u* will almost always produce a hard *g* sound. Therefore, the correct choice in this case is *juveniles*.

4. **feasible**. Remember that the letter *s* is sometimes pronounced with a *z* sound.

5. **access, account**. In these examples, the double *cs* are pronounced two different ways. However, if you break these words into roots and prefixes, the pronunciation becomes easier to understand. Both words have the same prefix: *ac-* meaning "to" or "toward." The root of *access* is *cess*, which is the same root found in the words *recess* and *incessant*. As you can see, this root is always pronounced with a soft *c* sound. The root of *account*, on the other hand, is pronounced with a hard *c* sound. So even though these words begin with the same letters, each retains the pronunciation of its original parts.

6. **gnashed**. The digraph *gn* can be found at the beginning or end of words. Other words that begin with the digraph *gn* are *gnat*, *gnu*, and *gnaw*.

7. **critiques**. The digraph *qu* can be pronounced (kw) or (k). In this situation, it is pronounced (k). *Critiques* are critical responses.

8. **succumb**. The digraph *mb* is always found at the end of words. Interestingly, there are no words that have an *emb* combination; so if the vowel is *e* and it has an *m* sound at the end, there will never be a silent *b*.

9. **knowledgeable**. The word *knowledgeable* has a digraph and a trigraph. Note that the silent *e* remains on the word *knowledge* even after adding the *-able* suffix. We'll cover this in further detail in the next chapter.

10. **flanked**. To *flank* a door means to protect it. Although the digraph *sh* would have made a word, it is doubtful that the guards would have *flashed* the palace doors!

11. My teacher gave me the ta**sk** of re**pl**acing the chips in the hamster's cage and di**sp**osing of his uneaten food.

12. **Thr**oughout history, the leaders who have shown re**sp**ect for their people have consi**st**ently been the most beloved.

13. Our host was extremely **gr**acious when I accidentally **br**oke her serving **pl**atter.

14. A **tr**emen**d**ous noise arose **fr**om the **cr**owd when the race cars **st**arted their engines.

15. As I watched the nature film, I was en**thr**alled by the de**str**uctive power of the **cr**ashing waves.

16. **indebted**. There are only two base words in the English language that end in *bt*: *debt* and *doubt*. (*Indebted* is *debt* with the prefix *in-* and the suffix *-ed*.) This would be a good time for a mnemonic!

17. **riled**. The mysterious *s* that can be found in the words *aisle* and *island* does not appear in every word with the (īl) sound. This is one of the cases where there is no silent *s*.

18. **flight**. Sometimes the words *flight* and *night* are spelled *flite* and *nite* in commercials and in company names. This doesn't make these spellings correct. *Flight* has a silent *gh*.

19. **hassle**. Although the word *hassle* rhymes with *castle*, *hassle* is spelled with a double *s* and *castle* is spelled with a silent *t*. The reasoning probably has something to do with ancient forms of these words. All we can do is trust our memories, in this case.

20. **drought**. Drought is another word with a silent *gh*. Remember that words with the *ough* combination have a number of different pronunciations.

Game Time: Spelling Jumble Solution

1

U	V	I	L	E	E	J	N

	J	U	V	E	N	I	(L)	E

I	L	R	D	E

	R	I	L	(E)	D

T	D	E	A	T	R	S	
	S	(T)	A	R	T	E	D

D	W	C	R	O	
	C	R	O	(W)	D

R	F	M	O	
	F	R	(O)	M

What gets wet the more it dries?

A (T)(O)(W)(E)(L)

2

C	U	A	C	T	O	N	
	(A)	C	C	O	U	N	T

E	E	S	C	P	T	R	
	R	E	S	(P)	E	C	T

K	A	S	T	
	T	A	(S)	K

G	T	L	I	F	H	
	F	L	I	G	H	(T)

U	S	C	M	C	U	B	
	S	U	C	C	U	(M)	B

What goes all around the world but stays in a corner?

A (S)(T)(A)(M)(P)

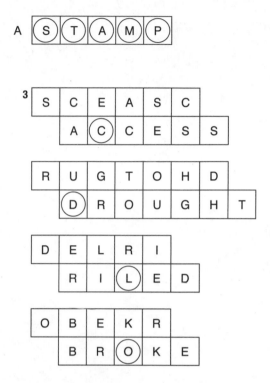

3

S	C	E	A	S	C

	A	(C)	C	E	S	S

R	U	G	T	O	H	D

	(D)	R	O	U	G	H	T

D	E	L	R	I

	R	I	(L)	E	D

O	B	E	K	R

	B	R	(O)	K	E

What can you catch but not throw?

A (C)(O)(L)(D)

4

T	E	R	P	T	L	A

	(P)	L	A	T	T	E	R

A	L	N	T	R	E	L	E	D	H

	E	N	T	H	R	A	L	L	(E)	D

A	S	U	O	G	C	I	R

	G	R	A	C	I	(O)	U	S

K	F	L	D	N	E	A

	F	L	A	Ⓝ	K	E	D

N	H	G	D	S	E	A

	Ⓖ	N	A	S	H	E	D

A	E	L	S	S	H

	H	A	S	Ⓢ	L	E

What is filled with holes but still holds water?

A Ⓢ Ⓟ Ⓞ Ⓝ Ⓖ Ⓔ

This Is How It Ends
Suffixes

While reading the last two chapters, you might have started to feel as though there are more exceptions in the English language than there are rules. It's true that when you look at words as nothing more than collections of vowels and consonants, it can be a little difficult to see the patterns. Certainly, memorizing the common vowel and consonant combinations can help you spell a large number of words, but these "rules" can only teach you a small part of the bigger picture. Your knowledge of the digraph *mb*, for instance, only comes in handy when you encounter words that end in an *m* sound.

Well, don't fret. Now that we're done looking at the sometimes overwhelming world of vowels and consonants, we can start to look at how parts of speech behave. And once we get into the different parts of speech, the rules become much more regular and easy to remember. In this chapter, you'll learn how words interact with suffix endings. But first, let's see how much you already know.

PRACTICE LAP

Choose the italicized word that is spelled correctly in each of the following sentences.

1. When I'm trying to fall asleep, it's (*comforting/comfortting*) to have my dog curled up at the end of the bed.

2. The party had been so highly (*enjoiable/enjoyable*) that he didn't want to leave.

3. Angelique has become the best (*runer/runner*) in the school.

4. Today in art class, we are (*drawwing/drawing*) still-life portraits.

5. The cowboy (*easily/easeily*) caught the calf in his lasso.

6. I feel like the longer the summer goes on, the (*lazier, lazyer*) I get.

7. My dad makes really (*tastey/tasty*) cornbread.

8. The mayor ran a very (*respectable/respecttable*) campaign for reelection.

9. Marco thought we would need only one bag of potato chips for the part, but his (*judgement/judgment*) was incorrect.

10. This year felt much (*hotter/hoter*) than last year.

Check your answers at the end of the chapter. How did you do?

PARTS OF SPEECH

Before we learn how endings work, we should do a quick refresher on the parts of speech to which endings can be added.

Part of Speech	Job	Examples	Common Endings
noun	names a person, place, thing, or idea	Jeremy, road, butter, theory	*-s, -es, -er, -ness, -age, -ant, -ent*
verb	names an action	run, play, float	*-s, -es, -ing, -ed, -ify, -en*

Part of Speech	Job	Examples	Common Endings
adjective	modifies a noun or pronoun	beautiful, funny, hungry	*-able, -ible, -ful, -ic, -less, -y*
adverb	modifies a verb, an adjective, another adverb, a clause, or a sentence	happily, very, now	*-ly*

When we're talking about endings, we're really talking about a few different things.

1. Plural endings: A **singular** noun is one person, place, thing, or idea, while a **plural** noun shows more than one person, place, thing, or idea. *Cougar* is singular, *cougars* is plural. Nouns are the only part of speech that have a plural ending. Plurals generally end in *-s* or *-es*, but there are some plurals that do not end in either. Plural endings will be discussed in Chapter 7.

2. Conjugation endings: Verbs are **conjugated** when they change tense. For example, *walk* is a verb in the present tense (i.e., I *walk* to school). *Walked* is a verb in the past tense (i.e., I *walked* to school), while *will walk* is the future tense (i.e., I *will walk* to school). There are other tenses, including the present continuous (I *am walking*), the past perfect (I *had walked* to the store before dinner), and the past perfect continuous (I *had been walking* for ten minutes when I arrived at the store). We'll examine verb conjugations in greater detail in Chapter 8.

3. Suffix endings: Technically, all letters added to the end of words are suffixes, including plural endings and conjugation endings. For the purpose of this book, though, we're going to think of suffix endings as endings that change a word from one part of speech to the other. For example, the word *teach* is a verb. Add the suffix ending *-er* to it, and it becomes a noun: *teacher*.

SUFFIX RULES

As you saw in the part of speech table, suffixes are categorized by the types of speech they represent. The suffix ending *-ment* is a noun ending. This means, if you see the suffix *-ment* on a word, that word will be a noun. This ending can only be added to verbs. To *state* something means to say it; the word *state* is a verb. A *statement* is something that is said; the word *statement* is a noun. So, in other words, the suffix turns the verb into a noun. In Appendix D you will find a list of the most common suffixes divided by the part of speech they represent.

There are six essential rules for adding suffix endings, and they are all pretty consistent. Learn these rules well; some of them will also help you later, when you are learning how to make singular nouns into plurals and conjugate verbs.

Suffix Rule #1: Consonant or Silent *e* + Consonant
If a suffix begins with a consonant, it can usually be attached to a base word that ends in a consonant or a silent *e* with no change to the base word or the suffix.
Examples:

➥ wise + -ly = *wisely*
➥ mechanic + -al = *mechanical*
➥ good + -ness = *goodness*

As with any good rule, there are always exceptions. A few words that end in silent *e* drop the *e* when adding suffix. For example, acknowledge + -ment = *acknowledgment*. Other common examples are *argument, awful, duly, judgment, ninth, truly, wholly,* and *wisdom.*

Suffix Rule #2: Silent *e* + Vowel
If a base word ends in a silent *e* and the suffix begins with a vowel, drop the silent *e* when adding the suffix.
Examples:

➥ type + -ist = *typist*
➥ drive + -able = *drivable*
➥ fortune + -ate = *fortunate*

The exception to this rule occurs when the suffixes *-able* or *-ous* are added to words that end in *g* + silent *e* or *c* + silent *e*. The silent *e* remains in these words as a reminder that the *g* and *c* sounds are soft.

Examples:

➡ courage + -ous = *courageous*
➡ notice + -able = *noticeable*
➡ outrage + -ous = *outrageous*

FUEL FOR THOUGHT

ADJECTIVES MODIFY NOUNS or pronouns. Words like *nice*, *pretty*, and *large* are all adjectives. Adverbs modify everything else: verbs, adjectives, other adverbs, clauses, and sentences. Adverbs answer the questions "How?" "Why?" "When?" "Where?" "In what way?" "How much?" "How often?" "Under what condition?" and "To what degree?" Words like *excitedly, today,* and *very* are all adverbs.

When adverbs modify verbs or adjectives, they often end in the suffix *-ly*. For example: "I walked *slowly*," "She chews *noisily*," or "We are *extremely* bored." You can't automatically assume that every word ending in *-ly* is an adverb; for example, *friendly, lonely,* and *lovely* are all adjectives.

Adverbs that end in *-ly* can be formed by adding *-ly* to adjectives (like *comfortable* or *poor*), present participles (*-ing* words like *surprising* or *trusting*), or past participles (*-ed* words like *assured* or *embarrassed*). There are a few special rules that pertain to suffixes ending in *-ly*:

1. **When the base word ends in *-able* or *-ible*, drop the final e and replace it with a *-y*.**
   Examples:
   ➡ terrible + -ly = *terribly*
   ➡ arguable + -ly = *arguably*
2. **When the base word ends in *-ic*, add *-ally*.**
   Examples:
   ➡ idiotic + -ly = *idiotically*
   ➡ emphatic + -ly = *emphatically*

Suffix Rule #3: When to change -*y* to an *i*

When base words end in a consonant + -*y* combination, change the -*y* to an *i* when adding suffixes. If the base word ends in a vowel + -*y* combination, keep the final -*y*.

Examples of words that end in consonant + -*y* combinations:

➡ beauty + -ful = *beautiful*
➡ busy + -ness= *business*
➡ marry + -age = *marriage*

Examples of words that end in vowel + -*y* combinations:

➡ destroy + -er = *destroyer*
➡ pay + -ment = *payment*
➡ buoy + -ant = *buoyant*

There is one very common exception to this rule: Something that happens every day happens *daily*, not *dayly*.

PRACTICE LAP

Choose the italicized word that is spelled correctly in each of the following sentences.

11. Most Americans receive (*unemploimen* /*unemployment*) insurance if they lose their jobs.

12. Kaia whistled (*happily*/*happyly*) to herself as she painted.

13. That has got to be the most (*pityful*/*pitiful*) looking dog I have ever seen.

14. The (*infamous*/*infameous*) bank robber struck again last night.

15. Shari built a website to bring (*awareness*/*awarness*) to the environmental challenges facing our generation.

16. My mother expressed (*annoiance/annoyance*) at having to take out the garbage when I forgot.

17. I have always been (*envious/envyous*) of Alain's natural athletic ability.

18. The coach said that missing the competition last weekend was absolutely (*inexcuseable/inexcusable*).

19. My grandmother's wedding ring is an (*irreplacable/irreplaceable*) treasure.

20. Put your tray on the (*conveier/conveyer*) belt when you are done eating.

Check your answers at the end of the chapter. How did you do?

Suffix Rule #4: Doubling Consonants

When a one-syllable base word ends in a consonant + vowel + consonant combination, double the final consonant when adding a suffix that begins with a vowel.

Examples:

➡ ship + -ing = *shipping*
➡ hot + -er = *hotter*
➡ rot + -en = *rotten*

Do not double the final consonant when adding a suffix that begins with a consonant, as in *shipment* or *hotly*.

Exceptions to this rule are words that end in *-w* or *-x*, such as *saw* (*sawing*) or *fix* (*fixable*).

Suffix Rule #5

When a base word of more than one syllable ends in the consonant + vowel + consonant combination *and* the accent is on the final syllable, double the final consonant when adding a suffix that begins with a vowel.

Examples:

➡ transmit + -er = *transmitter*
➡ begin + -ing = *beginning*
➡ excel + -ent = *excellent*

Exception: Add a *-k* after the *-c* when adding certain suffixes to words that end in *-c*. For example, panic + -y = *panicky*. The *-k* is added as a pronunciation guide.

CAUTION!

THE EXAMPLES MAY make it seem like you can add any suffix to any word, as long as you know the spelling rules. This is not the case. You can add the suffix *-ment* to the verbs *abandon*, *entertain* and *punish*, to make them into nouns, but if you stuck this suffix on the end of the verbs *smile* or *climb*, you'd end up with a pile of nonsensical mush. Make sure that the word you're creating with your new spelling knowledge actually *is* a word before you use it in a sentence!

Suffix Rule #6
When a base word ends in any other combination of vowels and consonants, do not double the final consonant when adding a suffix.
Examples:

➡ seat + -ing = *seating*
➡ breath + -able = *breathable*
➡ deduct + -ible = *deductible*

PRACTICE LAP

Choose the italicized word that is spelled correctly in each of the following sentences.

21. Follow my (*instructtions/instructions*) closely and we'll get these shelves built in no time.

22. The businessman was sentenced to jail for (*trafficcing/trafficking*) in stolen merchandise.

23. The farmer had to (*fatten/faten*) his pigs up for the county fair.

24. My doctor prescribed a muscle (*relaxxant/relaxant*) for my sore shoulder.

25. I got a (*referral/referal*) for an excellent piano teacher.

INSIDE TRACK

I HAVE NOT said a thing about spelling with prefixes yet, and this is a good thing. The reason why I haven't discussed prefixes is there is only one rule for prefixes, and it is consistent (almost) all the way across the board: *When adding a prefix to a base word, the base word does not change.*

Two vowels in a row? No problem! Re- + arrange = *rearrange*, pre- + order = *preorder*, and co- + operate = *cooperate*. What about two of the same consonants in a row? Go for it! Dis- + similar = *dissimilar*, il- + logical = *illogical*, and mis- + spell = *misspell*.

There is only one minor exception to know when it comes to prefixes, and it is the cause of many unnecessary spelling errors. *Drop the second l when adding the prefix all-*. Examples: all- + together = *altogether*, all- + ways = *always*, all- + mighty = *almighty*.

CROSSING THE FINISH LINE

In this chapter, we learned the six major rules for adding suffixes to base words, which are:

1. If a suffix begins with a consonant, it can usually be attached to base word that ends in a consonant or a silent *e* with no change to the base word or the suffix.
2. If a base word ends in a silent *e* and the suffix begins with a vowel, drop the silent *e* when adding the suffix.
3. When base words end in a consonant + *-y* combination, change the *-y* to an *i* when adding suffixes. If the base word ends in a vowel + *-y* combination, keep the final *y*.
4. When a one-syllable base word ends in a consonant + vowel + consonant combination, double the final consonant when adding a suffix that begins with a vowel.
5. When a base word of more than one syllable ends in the consonant + vowel + consonant combination *and* the accent is on the final syllable, double the final consonant when adding a suffix that begins with a vowel.
6. When a base word ends in any other combination of vowels and consonants, do not double the final consonant when adding a suffix.

We also learned the rules for adding the adverb suffix *-ly* to adjectives, present participles, and past participles:

1. When the base word ends in *-able* or *-ible*, drop the final *e* and replace it with a *-y*.
2. When the base word ends in *-ic*, add *-ally*.

GAME TIME: NOTABLE QUOTABLE

In the following groups of words, decide which word is spelled correctly. Then, take the letter next to that word and enter it into the corresponding blank. The final answer will spell a famous quote from baseball player, manager, and coach, Yogi Berra.

1. A inexkusable   B inexcusible   C inecscuable   D inexcusable

2. F drawing   G drauing   H drawwing   I drawng

3. J relaxent   K relaxant   L relaksant   M relaxsent

4. R unemploement   S unemplymint   T unemployment   U umeploiment

5. M tastey   N tasty   O tastie   P tastty

6. Q singulare   R singular   S singuler   T singullar

7. A respectable   B respectible   C respectabel   D respectibel

8. R easyly   S eseily   T easily   U easely

9. A fatten   B faten   C fattan   D faton

10. S irreplacable   T irreplaceable   U ireplacable   V irreplacible

11. G infamus   H enfamous   I infamous   J infameous

12. L commforting   M comfortting   N comforrting   O comforting

13. F anoyance   G annoyance   H annoiance   I annoyance

14. O conveier   P conveyor   Q convyer   R conveyer

15. N traffiking   O trafficking   P traficking   Q trafficing

16. F pitiful   G pityful   H pitifful   I pityfill

17. A referral   B referal   C referel   D refferal

18. D lazyer   E lazier   F lazeyer   G lazer

19. D awarness   E awareness   F awarenes   G awareniss

20. C instrutions   D instrucsions   E instructions   F intrucktions

21. R hapily   S happely   T happly   U happily

22. B enjoiable   C enjoyible   D enjoyabel   E enjoyable

23. N runer   O runner   P runer   Q ruuner

24. W plurel   X plurl   Y plural   Z pllural

25. I envyous   J envius   K envious   L enveous

26. G conjuggate   H conjugate   I conjugete   J connjugate

27. I judgment   J jujement   K judgement   L jugement

28. Q hoter   R hottir   S hotter   T hottar

___ ___   ___ ___ ___   ___ ___ ___   ___   ___ ___ ___ ___

27   2   24   15   21   28   22   18   7   16   12   6   25

___ ___   ___ ___ ___   ___ ___ ___ ___   ,   ___ ___ ___ ___   ___ ___ .

13   5   8   26   19   14   23   9   1   10   17   3   20   11   4

CHAPTER 6 WORD LIST

adjective (ăd´jəkt-ĭv)
adverb (ăd´vərb)
annoyance (ə-noi´əns)
awareness (ə-wâr´nəss)
comforting (kŭm´fərt-ĭng)
conjugate (kŏn´jə-gāt)
conveyer (kŭn-vā´ər)

drawing (drô´ ĭng)

easily (ē´zə-lē)

enjoyable (ĕn-joi´əbəl)

envious (ĕn´vē-əs)

fatten (făt´ən)

happily (hăp´ə-lē)

hotter (hŏt´ər)

inexcusable (ĭn-ĕk-skyû´zə-bəl)

infamous (ĭn´fəm-əs)

instructions (ĭn-strŭk-shənz)

irreplaceable (ĭr-rə-plās´ə-bəl)

judgment (jŭj´mənt)

lazier (lā´zē-ər)

noun (nown)

pitiful (pĭt´ə-fəl)

plural (plərəl)

referral (rē-fər´əl)

relaxant (rē-lak´zənt)

respectable (rē-spĕkt´ə-bəl)

runner (rŭn-ər)

singular (sĭng´gyû-lər)

tasty (tăst´ē)

trafficking (tră´fĭk-ĭng)

unemployment (ŭn-əm-ploi´mənt)

verb (vŭrb)

ANSWERS

1. **comforting.** If a word ends in anything besides a consonant + vowel + consonant combination, the final consonant will not be doubled. (suffix rule #6)

2. **enjoyable.** Words that end in vowel + -y combinations keep the final y when adding suffixes. (suffix rule #3)

3. **runner.** If a one-syllable word begins with a consonant + vowel + consonant combination, the final consonant will be doubled when adding suffixes. (suffix rule #4)

4. **drawing.** One-syllable words that end in -*w* do not double the final consonant. (exception to suffix rule #4)

5. **easily.** When the base word of an adverb ends in -*y*, change the -*y* to an *i* before adding -*ly* (suffix rule #3)

6. **lazier.** On words that end in consonant + -*y*, change the final *y* to an *i* when adding suffixes. (suffix rule #3)

7. **tasty.** Base words that end in a silent *e* drop the final *e* before adding suffixes that begin with vowels. (suffix rule #2)

8. **respectable.** Words that end in two consonants should not double the final consonant. (suffix rule #6)

9. **judgment.** Most words that end in -*ge* keep the final *e* as a pronunciation guide; *judgment* is an exception. (This is actually an exception to the exception to suffix rule #2.)

10. **hotter.** One-syllable words with consonant + vowel + consonant combinations get the final consonant doubled before adding suffixes that start with vowels. (suffix rule #4)

11. **unemployment.** Words that end in vowel + -*y* combinations keep the final *y* when adding suffixes. (suffix rule #3)

12. **happily.** When the base word of adverbs ends in -*y*, change the -*y* to an *i* before adding -*ly* (suffix rule #3)

13. **pitiful.** On words that end in consonant + -*y*, change the final *y* to an *i* when adding suffixes. (suffix rule #3)

14. **infamous.** Base words that end in a silent *e* drop the final *e* before adding suffixes that begin with vowels. (suffix rule #2)

15. **awareness.** Most words that end in silent *e* keep the silent *e* when adding suffixes that begin with consonants. (suffix rule #1)

16. **annoyance.** Words that end in vowel + -*y* combinations keep the final *y* when adding suffixes. (suffix rule #3)

17. **envious.** On words that end in consonant + -*y*, change the final *y* to an *i* when adding suffixes. (suffix rule #3)

18. **inexcusable.** Base words that end in a silent *e* drop the final *e* before adding suffixes. (suffix rule #2)

19. **irreplaceable.** Words that end in -*ce* or -*ge* keep the final *e* when adding suffixes. (exception to suffix rule #2)

20. **conveyer.** Words that end in vowel + -*y* combinations keep the final *y* when adding suffixes. (suffix rule #3)

21. **instructions.** When a base word does not end in a consonant + vowel + consonant combination, do not double the final consonant before adding a suffix. (suffix rule #6)

22. **trafficking.** When adding a suffix that begins with a vowel to a word that ends in *-ic*, add a *-k* before the suffix. (exception to suffix rule #5)

23. **fatten.** When a one-syllable base word ends in a consonant + vowel + consonant combination, double the final consonant when adding a suffix that begins with a vowel. (suffix rule #4)

24. **relaxant.** Words that end in *-x* or *-w* do not get doubled when added to suffixes that begin with vowels. (exception to suffix rule #4)

25. **referral.** When a base word of more than one syllable ends in the consonant + vowel + consonant combination *and* the accent is on the final syllable, double the final consonant when adding the suffix. (suffix rule #5)

Game Time: Notable Quotable Solution

1. D inexcusable
2. F drawing
3. K relaxant
4. T unemployment
5. N tasty
6. R singular
7. A respectable
8. T easily
9. A fatten
10. T irreplaceable
11. I infamous
12. O comforting
13. G annoyance
14. R conveyer
15. O trafficking
16. F pitiful
17. A referral
18. E lazier
19. E awareness
20. E instructions

21. U happily
22. E enjoyable
23. O runner
24. Y plural
25. K envious
26. H conjugate
27. I judgment
28. S hotter

Quote:

I F   Y O U   S E E   A   F O R K
___ ___   ___ ___ ___   ___ ___ ___   ___   ___ ___ ___ ___
27 2   24 15 21   28 22 18   7   16 12   6 25

I N   T H E   R O A D ,   T A K E   I T .
___ ___   ___ ___ ___   ___ ___ ___ ___   ___ ___ ___ ___   ___ ___
13   5   8 26 19   14 23   9   1   10 17   3 20   11   4

7
I'll Take Two
Plurals

By this point in your school career, you probably know that singular nouns show *one* thing and plural nouns show *more than one* thing. You've probably known since the first or second grade that the plural of *man* is *men*, or the plural of *child* is *children*. Most likely, you don't even need to think about what the plural of *man* or *child* is; after years of usage, it has become something that's simply there in your mind.

If the only plurals you ever used were common, everyday words like *men* or *children*, you'd be just fine right now and we wouldn't need to spend a chapter talking about the rules for pluralizing. As your vocabulary develops, however, you'll learn new words that don't seem to fit into any of the rules you currently know. For example, you might know that *data* are bits of information, but did you know that the word *data* is plural? A single bit of *data* is known as *datum*. An *analysis* is a study of something; the plural of *analysis* is *analyses*. You probably don't use these words in your everyday life just yet, but you may someday. When you do, it will be helpful to know the rules for pluralizing them; if you go around to your fellow scientists talking about all the datums in your analysises, they might just send you straight back to school!

PRACTICE LAP

Write the plural form of each of the following words.

1. child   _____

2. tomato   _____

3. lunch   _____

4. wolf   _____

5. ankle   _____

6. pantry   _____

7. medium   _____

8. knife   _____

9. sweater   _____

10. parenthesis   _____

Check your answers at the end of the chapter. How did you do?

PLURAL RULES

There are five main rules for turning singular nouns into plural nouns. Luckily, 90% of the words you use on a daily basis will follow the simplest rule, Rule #1.

Plural Rule #1: Add -s or–es
Add -*s* to most words to make them plural. If a word ends in -*s*, -*x*, -*z*, -*sh*, or -*ch*, add -*es*.

Examples:

➡ plane + -s = *planes*
➡ tax + -es = *taxes*
➡ watch + -es = *watches*

The reason why *-es* is added in certain situations is a matter of pronunciation. The consonants *s*, *x*, and *z* all end in a hissing sound. It would be difficult to hear an *s* at the end of a word like *tax*, so instead, we add an *-es*. The same holds true for *-ch* and *-sh* endings; it sounds awkward to go from the *sh* and *ch* sounds right into an *-s*, so we add an *-es* to make pronunciation easier. There are two notable exceptions to this rule. One is the word *stomach*, the plural of which is *stomachs*. This is because the *ch* sound in stomach is pronounced with a hard *k* sound instead of the soft *ch* sound, and it is easy to pronounce an *s* after this sound. The other is the word *ox*. The plural of *ox* is *oxen*. Don't ask us why. It just is.

Plural Rule #2: Words that end in -o
If a word ends in a *vowel* + *-o* combination, add *-s* to make the plural. If a word ends in a *consonant* + *-o* combination, add *-es*.
Examples:

➡ duo + -s = *duos*
➡ trio + -s = *trios*
➡ moo + -s = *moos*
➡ tornado + -es = *tornadoes*
➡ torpedo + -es = *torpedoes*
➡ potato + -es = *potatoes*

There are a few exceptions to this rule. The following consonant + *-o* words require only an *-s*:

> albino (*albinos*), armadillo (*armadillos*), bronco (*broncos*), logo (*logos*), memo (*memos*), silo (*silos*). Musical instruments and terms also only take an *–s*: alto (*altos*), banjo (*banjos*), piano (*pianos*), solo (*solos*), and soprano (*sopranos*).

CAUTION!

THERE ARE a handful of common words that are used only in the plural form. You can wear a pair of *pants*, but you can't wear a singular *pant*. You can use a pair of *scissors*, but you can't just use a *scissor*. (You might hear some people referring to "a scissor," particularly if you live on the East Coast . . . technically, the term is not correct.)

Other words that don't have a singular form include *cattle*, *clothes*, *eaves*, *pliers*, *shorts*, and *trousers*. Interestingly, the words *folk* and *folks* are *both* plurals, without any singular form! The sentences "Many *folk* like spaghetti" and "Many *folks* like spaghetti" are both grammatically correct.

Plural Rule #3: Words that end in -y

When a noun ends in a *vowel* + -y ending, add an -s to form the plural. When a noun ends in a *consonant* + -y ending, change the -y to an i and add -es.

Examples:

➡ tray + -s = *trays*
➡ fly + -es = *flies*
➡ penny + -es = *pennies*
➡ candy + -es = *candies*

Plural Rule #4: Words that end in -f and -fe

For most words that end in -f or -fe, change the f or -fe to a v, then add -es.

Examples:

➡ elf + -es = *elves*
➡ life + -es = *lives*
➡ shelf + -es = *shelves*

Notable exceptions to this rule include nouns that end in double *f* such as *sheriffs, cuffs,* and *plaintiffs,* and the words *beliefs, briefs, chefs, chiefs, gulfs, roofs,* and *safes.*

INSIDE TRACK

IF YOU'RE HAVING trouble remembering the exceptions to the spelling rules, keep in mind that there is strength in numbers. By this, I mean that it is sometimes easier to remember several exceptions with similar patterns than it is to remember each one individually. For example, three words that don't follow the "change the *-f* to a *v*" rule are *beliefs, briefs,* and *chiefs.* It is more likely you'll remember each of these words if you think of them as a small group of words ending in *-iefs* than if you picture each word as being completely unique.

Plural Rule #5: Hyphenated Words
When pluralizing hyphenated words, add the *-s* to the word that is being pluralized.

Examples:

➡ ex-husband + -s = *ex-husbands*
➡ father-in-law + -s = *fathers-in-law*
➡ court-martial + -s = *courts-martial*

This is also true for certain unhyphenated terms that are used as a single noun. For instance, the plural of attorney general is *attorneys general.*

PRACTICE LAP
Before we get to the list of strange rules and total exceptions, let's see how well you can use some of the rules we've learned so far. Choose the correct spelling of the italicized word in each of the following sentences.

11. I helped my little sister build a fort out of cardboard (*boxes/boxs*).

12. These (*earmuves/earmuffs*) may look silly, but they really keep my ears warm!

13. We visited two different film (*studios/studioes*) on our vacation to Hollywood.

14. Norman's grandfather earned his (*richs/riches*) through many years of hard work.

15. "Be very quiet," Aladdin said. "There are (*thieves/thiefs*) in the cave."

16. Henry's (*daughters-in-law/daughter-in-laws*) are both less than 35 years old.

17. "Close the (*hatches/hatchs*)!" shouted the submarine commander.

18. I wasn't sure how to choose from the selection of (*modems/modemes*) at the electronics store.

19. Six kids went home with (*rashs/rashes*) before they discovered that the woods behind the school were filled with poison oak.

20. The (*navies/navys*) of the allied countries are stationed in the same port.

Check your answers at the end of the chapter. How did you do?

Plural Rule #6: Strange plurals—technical words

Some technical words that end in *-um* or *-on* change the *-um* or *-on* to an *a* when forming plurals.

Examples:

Some words that end in *-us* change the *-us* to an *i*.
Some words that end in *-is* change the *-is* to *-es*.
Some words that end in *-ex* or *-ix* change the *-ex* or *-ix* to *-ices*.

These are very strange rules, indeed, but there is a small bit of logic beyond them. Some technical words that come directly from Latin or Greek roots make their plurals the same way they would be made in these original languages. Technical words, in this case, are words that are used in the sciences. Examples of these words can be found in the following tables.

Words that end in -um *or* -on

Singular	Plural
curriculum	curricula
datum	data
medium	media
stratum	strata
criterion	criteria
phenomenon	phenomena

Words that end in -us

Singular	Plural
alumnus	alumni
focus	foci
nucleus	nuclei
thesaurus	thesauri

Words that end in -ex *or* -ix

Singular	Plural
appendix	appendices
apex	apices
matrix	matrices

Words that end in -is

Singular	Plural
analysis	analyses
basis	bases
hypothesis	hypotheses
oasis	oases
parenthesis	parentheses
thesis	theses

The ending to these words is pronounced with a long *e* sound, as in (ə-năl'ə-sēs) (*analyses*) or ō as in (ā'sēs) (*oases*).

Plural Rule #7: Words without plurals

The plural form of some animal names is the same as the singular form. You can see one *fish* or many *fish*. Other animal names that have the same singular and plural forms include:

➥ bison
➥ deer
➥ moose
➥ sheep

The words *series* and *species* are also the same in the singular and plural.

Plural Rule #8: Irregular plurals

Some words don't follow any rules. Okay, this is not so much a rule as it is a list of words whose plurals just don't make any sense. All you can do with these words is—you guessed it—memorize them.

Irregular Plurals

Singular	Plural
alga	algae
apparatus	apparatuses
beau	beaux
child	children
die	dice
foot	feet
genus	genera
goose	geese
louse	lice
man	men
mouse	mice
nebula	nebulae
person	people
tableau	tableaux
that	those
tooth	teeth
this	these

Singular	Plural
vertebra	vertebrae
vita	vitae
woman	women

Even with these words, you will see some patterns that can help you put the words into groups. For example, a few different words that end in -*a* add an -*e* when forming plurals, and all of the words in the list that have *oo* in the middle change the *oo* to an *ee* in the plural form. (Be careful you don't do the same thing with *moose*, which is the same in its singular and plural forms. You would see a bunch of *moose*, not a bunch of *meese*!)

Also, keep in mind that although the plural of *man* is *men* and the plural of *woman* is *women*, the plural of *human* is *humans*.

FUEL FOR THOUGHT

SOME WORDS CAN be pluralized in a few different ways. In many cases, common words that follow irregular rules of pluralization can also be pluralized according to the -*s* and -*es* rule. Words that have two different accepted plural forms include:

Singular	Plural
antenna	antennae, antennas
appendix	appendices, appendixes
buffalo	buffalos, buffaloes
cactus	cacti, cactuses
dwarf	dwarfs, dwarves
fungus	fungi, funguses
hippopotamus	hippopotami, hippopotamuses
hoof	hoofs, hooves
index	indices, indexes
radius	radii, radiuses
scarf	scarfs, scarves

Singular	Plural
syllabus	syllabi, syllabuses
symposium	symposia, symposiums
zero	zeros, zeroes

PRACTICE LAP

Use your knowledge of the pluralizing rules to find the plurals of the following words.

21. tributary   _____

22. stimulus   _____

23. politician   _____

24. ovum   _____

25. buffalo   _____

26. paralysis   _____

27. loaf   _____

28. umbrella   _____

29. index   _____

30. vertebra   _____

Check your answers at the end of the chapter. How did you do?

CROSSING THE FINISH LINE

In this chapter, we studied the eight rules for turning singular nouns into plural nouns, which are:

1. Add *-s* to most words to make them plural. If a word ends in *-s, -x, -z, -sh,* or *-ch*, add *-es.*
2. If a word ends in a vowel + *-o* combination, add *-s* to make the plural. If a word ends in a consonant + *-o* combination, add–*es.*
3. When a noun ends in a vowel + *-y* ending, add an *-s* to form the plural. When a noun ends in a consonant + *-y* ending, change the *-y* to an i and add *-es.*
4. For most words that end in *-f* or *-fe*, change the *f* or *-fe* to a *v*, then add *-es.*
5. When pluralizing hyphenated words, add the *-s* to the word that is being pluralized.
6. Some technical words that end in *-um* or *-on* change the *-um* or *-on* to an *-a* when forming plurals. Some words that end in *-us* change the *-us* to an *-i*. Some words that end in *-is* change the *-is* to an *-es*. Some words that end in *-ex* or *-ix* change the *-ex* or *-ix* to *-ices.*
7. The plural form of some animal names is the same as the singular form.
8. Some words don't follow any rules.

We also learned that some words such as *pants*, *scissors*, and *cattle* don't have singular forms, and that other words, like *buffalos/buffaloes*, have two accepted plural forms.

GAME TIME: SPELLING JUMBLE

The following boxes feature jumbled-up words from the Chapter 7 word list. Write the unscrambled words in the empty boxes. Then unscramble the circled letters to find the answer to each riddle.

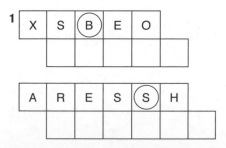

A	M	L	S	U	L	B	E	R
						◯		

M	D	E	A	I
	◯			

What gets bigger the more you take from it?

A ◯◯◯◯

2
I	E	N	S	V	K
◯					

I	C	R	H	N	L	D	E
◯							

C	S	D	E	I	I	N
				◯		

E	R	A	S	P	S	L	Y	A
				◯				

O	A	E	S	V	L
	◯				

What has two hands but can't clap?

A ◯◯◯◯◯

3

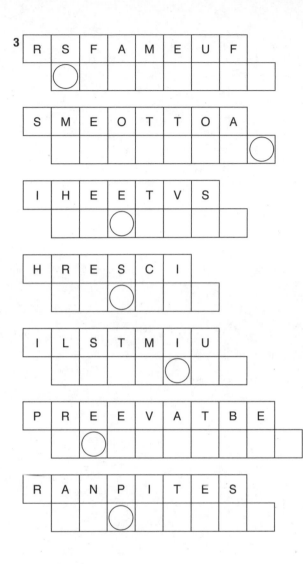

R S F A M E U F

S M E O T T O A

I H E E T V S

H R E S C I

I L S T M I U

P R E E V A T B E

R A N P I T E S

What can you break by saying its name?

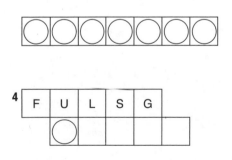

4

F U L S G

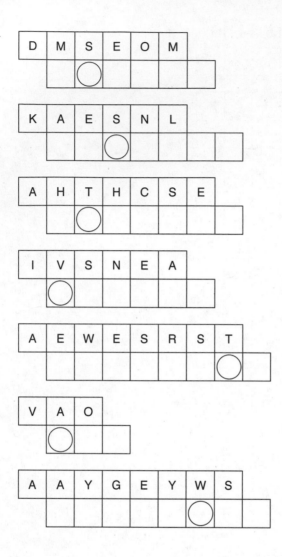

What jumps when it walks and sits when it stands?

A

Chapter 7 Word List

ankle (ăng′kəl)
boxes (bŏk′zəz)
buffaloes (bŭf′ə-lōz)
children (chĭl′drən)
earmuffs (îr′mŭfs)
gateways (gāt′wāz)

gulfs (gŭlfs)

hatches (hă´chəz)

indices (ĭn´də-sēz)

knives (nīvz)

loaves (lōvz)

lunches (lŭn-chəz)

media (mē´dē´ə)

modems (mō´dəmz)

navies (nā´vēz)

ova (ō-və)

pantries (păn´trēz)

paralyses (pər-ăl´ə-sēz)

parentheses (pər-ĕn´*th*ə-sēz)

politicians (pŏl-ə-tĭ-shənz)

rashes (răsh´əz)

riches (rĭch´əz)

stepbrothers (stĕp´brŭ-*th*ərz)

stimuli (stĭm´yû-lī)

studios (stü´dē-ōz)

sweaters (swĕt-ərz)

thieves (thēvz)

tomatoes (təm-ā´tōz)

umbrellas (üm-brĕl-əz)

vertebrae (vərt´ə-brā)

ANSWERS

1. **children.** *Children* is one of the words that doesn't follow any rules. (See the table for rule #8.)

2. **tomatoes.** If a word ends in a consonant + *-o* combination, add *-es* to make the plural. (Rule #2)

3. **lunches.** If a word ends in *-s, -x, -z, -sh,* or *-ch,* add *-es* when making the plural. (Rule #1)

4. **wolves.** For most words that end in *-f* or *-fe,* change the *-f* or *-fe* to a *v,* then add *-es.* (Rule #4)

5. **ankles.** Add *-s* to most words to make them plural. (Rule #1)

6. **pantries.** When a noun ends in a consonant + -*y* combination, change the -y to an i and add -*es* to form the plural. (Rule #3)

7. **media.** Some technical words that end in -*um* change the -*um* to an -*a* when forming plurals. (Rule #6)

8. **knives.** For most words that end in -*f* or -*fe*, change the -*f* or -*fe* to a *v*, then add -*es*. (Rule #4)

9. **sweaters.** Add -*s* to most words to make them plural. (Rule #1)

10. **parentheses.** Some words that end in -*is* change the -*is* to an -*es* when forming plurals (Rule #6)

11. **boxes.** If a word ends in -*s*, -*x*, -*z*, -*sh*, or -*ch*, add -*es* when making the plural. (Rule #1)

12. **earmuffs.** Most words that end in -*ff* add -*s* when forming the plural. (See the exception to rule #4)

13. **studios.** If a word ends in a *vowel* + -*o* combination, add -*s* to make the plural. (Rule #2)

14. **riches.** If a word ends in -*s*, -*x*, -*z*, -*sh*, or -*ch*, add -*es* when making the plural. (Rule #1)

15. **thieves.** For most words that end in -*f* or -*fe*, change the -*f* or -*fe* to a *v*, then add -*es*. (Rule #4.)

16. **daughters-in-law.** To make hyphenated words plural, add an -*s* to the word that is being pluralized. (Rule #5)

17. **hatches.** If a word ends in -*s*, -*x*, -*z*, -*sh*, or -*ch*, add -*es* when making the plural. (Rule #1)

18. **modems.** Add -*s* to most words to make them plural. (Rule #1)

19. **rashes.** If a word ends in -*s*, -*x*, -*z*, -*sh*, or -*ch*, add -*es* when making the plural. (Rule #1)

20. **navies.** When a noun ends in a consonant+ -*y* combination, change *y* to an *i* and add -*es* to form the plural. (Rule #3)

21. **tributaries.** When a noun ends in a consonant + -*y* combination, change the -*y* to an *i* and add -*es* to form the plural. (Rule #3)

22. **stimuli.** Some words that end in -*us* change the -*us* to an -*i* when forming plurals. (Rule #6)

23. **politicians.** Add -*s* to most words to make them plural. (Rule #1)

24. **ova.** Some technical words that end in -*um* change the -*um* to an -*a* when forming plurals. (Rule #6)

25. **buffalos, buffaloes.** Most words that end in a consonant + -*o* combination add an -*es* when forming the plural. *Buffalo* is one of the rare

exceptions that can be pluralized either way. (See the *Fuel for Thought* box in this chapter.)

26. **paralyses.** Some words that end in *-is* change the *-is* to an *-es* when forming plurals. (Rule #6)

27. **loaves.** For most words that end in *-f* or *-fe*, change the *-f* or *-fe* to a *v*, then add *-es*. (Rule #4)

28. **umbrellas.** Add *-s* to most words to make them plural. (Rule #1)

29. **indices, indexes.** Although most technical words that end in *-ix* change the *-ix* to *-ices* when forming the plural, the plural off *index* can be spelled two different ways. (See the *Fuel for Thought* box in this chapter.)

30. **vertebrae.** Some words don't obey any rules. (Rule #8)

Game Time: Spelling Jumble Solution

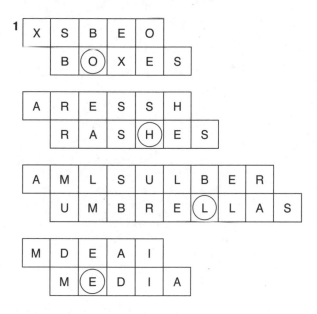

What gets bigger the more to take from it?

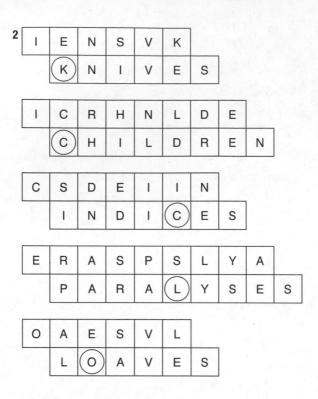

What has two hands but can't clap?

A (C)(L)(O)(C)(K)

I	L	S	T	M	I	U

	S	T	I	M	U	Ⓛ	I

P	R	E	E	V	A	T	B	E

	V	Ⓔ	R	T	E	B	R	A	E

R	A	N	P	I	T	E	S

	P	A	Ⓝ	T	R	I	E	S

What can you break by saying its name?

Ⓢ	Ⓘ	Ⓛ	Ⓔ	Ⓝ	Ⓒ	Ⓔ

4

F	U	L	S	G

	Ⓖ	U	L	F	S

D	M	S	E	O	M

	M	Ⓞ	D	E	M	S

K	A	E	S	N	L

	A	N	Ⓚ	L	E	T	S

A	H	T	H	C	S	E

	H	Ⓐ	T	C	H	E	S

I	V	S	N	E	A

	Ⓝ	A	V	I	E	S

A	E	W	E	S	R	S	T

	S	W	E	A	T	E	Ⓡ	S

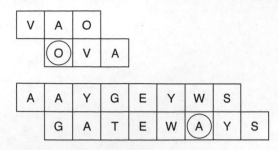

What jumps when it walks and sits when it stands?

Feeling Tense?
Verb Conjugation

***T**he dictionary defines* a verb as "the part of speech that expresses existence, action, or occurrence." This definition does not quite capture the extreme importance of verbs to our language and our way of thinking. If we didn't have verbs, we would have no way of expressing what we were doing, where we were going, what we were thinking, or who we are. If there were no verbs, we would be unable to talk about the past or the future. We could point to objects and say their names, but this conversation would probably get pretty boring after a while. Without verbs, we couldn't even acknowledge that we didn't have much to talk about, since *acknowledge* and *talk* are verbs themselves!

The rules for conjugating verbs can be a difficult thing to understand, mostly because there are so many verbs that are exceptions. As we take a look at verb tenses and forms, however, you will see some of the same spelling patterns that you've already learned while studying suffix and plural endings. The rules for spelling the past tense of regular verbs, for instance, are almost exactly the same as the rules for making the plural forms of regular nouns, except instead of using the letters *-s* or *-es*, you use the letters *-d* or *-ed*.

VERB FORMS

Every verb in the English language has potentially five different spelling forms: **present tense form**, **third person singular present tense form**, **past tense form**, **present participle form**, and **past participle form**. One verb, *be*, has a few additional forms.

Before we look at the rules for conjugating verbs, let's take a quick look at the five major spelling forms.

Form #1: Present tense

The present tense is the tense of a verb used to show something happening right now, or an existing state of being. It is also known as the **base** form. The present tense is used with all subjects except third person singular, including first person singular (*I*), first person plural (*we*), second person (*you*), and third person plural (*they, dogs, skies, buildings,* and so on).

Here are some examples of present tense verbs.

➡ drive: I **drive**.
➡ love: We **love** candy.
➡ run: The dogs **run** fast.

Form #2: Third person singular present tense

A third person singular subject is the subject he, she, it, or any other singular noun, like *dog, sky,* or *building*.

Here are some examples of present tense verbs with third person singular subjects.

➡ drive: He **drives**.
➡ love: She **loves** candy.
➡ run: The dog **runs** fast.

Form #3: Past tense

The past tense of a verb shows an action that happened in the past. For any given verb, all subjects (I, you, he, she, it, we, they, or any singular or plural subject) will take the same past tense. The verb *be* is the only exception.

For example:

➡ drive: I **drove**. He **drove**. They **drove**.
➡ love: We **loved** candy. He **loved** candy. They **loved** candy.
➡ run: The dogs **ran** fast. I **ran** fast. He **ran** fast.

Form #4: Present participle

A participle is a verb that is used in a multipart verb tense as an adjective or a noun. The present participle is used to show that something is happening right now. In the sentence "They are running," the word *running* is a participle. All present participles end in the letters *-ing*. The verb in a sentence with a present participle is called a **helping verb**, and it will always be a form of the word *be*.

   Examples:

➡ drive: I am **driving**. (*Am* is the helping verb.)
➡ love: We are **loving** candy. (*Are* is the helping verb.)
➡ run: The dogs are **running** fast. (*Are* is the helping verb.)

Form #5: Past participle

Past participles are used to show a past or completed action, or as an adjective. The verb in a sentence with a past participle is also called a helping verb, and it will always be a form of the word *have*. In some cases, the past participle will be the same as the past tense of a verb.

   Examples:

➡ drive: I have **driven** before. (*Have* is the helping verb.)
➡ love: We have **loved** candy in the past. (*Have* is the helping verb.)
➡ run: The dogs have **run** fast before, but today they are slow. (*Have* is the helping verb.)

   Regular past participles end in *-ed*, but as the three examples show, there are a lot of everyday verbs that have irregular past participle forms.

PRACTICE LAP

In the following sentences, decide whether the verb form is (1) present tense form, (2) third person singular present tense form, (3) past tense form, (4) present participle form, (5) past participle form. Determine the form of the verb in each sentence and write the number in the space following the sentence.

1. The Hendersons **fix** dinner while watching television. _____

2. Helene and Keisha **wanted** an ice cream cake at their party. _____

3. You should have **taken** art classes this year. _____

4. "What's wrong?" **asks** Jake. "Are you upset?" _____

5. This morning, Jose **tripped** on the way to school. _____

6. The class **laughed** at Ricardo's hilarious presentation. _____

7. Trish has been **smiling** more often since she got her braces taken off. _____

8. My dad is **driving** to work this morning. _____

9. Virginia **waits** at the end of her driveway for the school bus.

10. Mr. Lin has **played** piano for almost 17 years. _____

Check your answers at the end of the chapter. How did you do?

HOW TO CONJUGATE REGULAR VERBS

In the last section, we learned that all verbs (except *be*) potentially have five spelling forms. These spelling forms can be used together with other verbs to create all the different verb tenses. The future tense, for instance, is created by combining the verb *will* + *present tense form*, as in "I *will go* to the movies tomorrow," or "She *will enjoy* her summer vacation." Entire books have been written about verb tenses, so we won't have enough time to cover all the different combinations of verbs in this book. You will, however, learn to spell the five different forms of verbs that are used when constructing sentences.

When looking at the verb endings, keep in mind that verb endings are suffixes that follow the spelling rules covered in Chapter 6. To refresh your memory, these rules are:

➡ If a suffix begins with a consonant, it can usually be attached to base word that ends in a consonant or a silent *e* with no change to the base word or the suffix.

➡ If a base word ends in a silent *e* and the suffix begins with a vowel, drop the silent *e* when adding the suffix.

➡ When base words end in a consonant + *-y* combination, change the *-y* to an *i* when adding suffixes. If the base word ends in a vowel + *-y* combination, keep the final*-y*.

➡ When a one-syllable base word ends in a consonant + vowel + consonant combination, double the final consonant when adding a suffix that begins with a vowel.

➡ When a base word of more than one syllable ends in the consonant + vowel + consonant combination *and* the accent is on the final syllable, double the final consonant when adding a suffix that begins with a vowel.

➡ When a base word ends in any other combination of vowels and consonants, do not double the final consonant when adding a suffix.

Rule #1: Present tense form

The present tense (or base) form of a verb is the infinitive of the verb minus the word *to*.

This rule is nice and easy, because it doesn't require you to do a darn thing. The basic form of a verb is known as the **infinitive** form. *To bathe*, *to fly*, and *to imagine* are all infinitive forms. The present tense form of any verb is the infinitive without the word *to*. So the present tense of the infinitive *to bathe* is simply *bathe*. With the exception of *to be* and the third person singular present tense form (see Rule #2), this rule holds true for all verbs, regular or irregular; now *that's* the kind of rule we like!

Rule #2: Third person singular present tense form

Add *-s* to make the third person singular present tense form. If the verb ends in a consonant + *-y* combination, change the *-y* to an *i* and add *-es*. Examples:

➡ heal + -s = *heals*. The doctor *heals* his patients.
➡ file + -s = *files*. My sister *files* her nails when they look ragged.

➡ employ + -s = *employs*. General Motors *employs* workers from all over the world.

➡ pry + -es = *pries*. The plumber *pries* the faucet from the sink.

This rule should be easy to remember, because it's the same as pluralizing nouns. The rule is the same for all regular and irregular verbs.

CAUTION!

YOU MAY HAVE been taught that there are *singular* verbs and *plural* verbs. This is a common way of explaining the difference between the present form of a verb that is used with the various kinds of nouns. This description, however, is somewhat confusing and incorrect.

First of all, the words *singular* and *plural* have pretty rigid definitions: *Singular* means "one," and *plural* means "more than one." A singular noun would be an *apple*, and a plural noun would be two or three or 50,000 *apples*. But what is a plural of a verb? Could you have two "enjoys" or 50,000 "waits"?

Second of all, one would think that a singular form of a verb would be used with all singular subjects, but that is not the case. What is sometimes taught as the singular form of a verb is *only* used with third person singular subjects like *he, she,* or *it*. But *I* and *you* are singular subjects as well, which, for some unexplained reason, take the plural form of a verb.

Third, it is hopelessly confusing that the singular form of verbs has an -*s*, while the plural form of verbs does *not* have an -*s*.

For these reasons, I've chosen to refer to the two different forms of present tense verbs as simply *present tense form* and *third person present tense form*. If you have learned differently and would like to think of the verbs as singular and plural forms, that's fine; just don't forget that some singular subjects take plural verbs!

Rule #3: Past tense form

Add -*d* or -*ed* to make the past tense form.

Examples:

➥ telephone + -ed = *telephoned*. Susan *telephoned* late last night.
➥ grill + -ed = *grilled*. We *grilled* hamburgers out on the porch.
➥ sway + -ed = *swayed*. The dancers *swayed* to the music.
➥ imply + -ed = *implied*. Antonio *implied* that he didn't like baseball.
➥ tan + -ed = *tanned*. The model *tanned* on the beach. (In this case, the *n* is doubled.)
➥ repel + -ed = *repelled*. The army *repelled* the invaders from the castle. (In this case, the *l* is doubled.)

Rule #4: Present participle form

Add -*ing* to form the present participle.

Examples:

➥ fly + -ing = *flying*. I'd love to go *flying* in a hot air balloon someday.
➥ stare + -ing = *staring*. Melissa keeps *staring* out the window. (In this case, the *e* is dropped.)
➥ rub + -ing = *rubbing*. The massage therapist is *rubbing* my sore ankle. (In this case, the *b* is doubled.)
➥ refer + -ing = *referring*. Are you *referring* to the solar eclipse that happened last night? (In this case, the *r* is doubled.)
➥ All verbs regular and irregular follow this rule for forming the present participle.

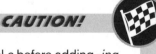

CAUTION!

Exceptions to Rule #4: You must drop a final *e* before adding -*ing* to form the present participle. There are a few exceptions to this rule. You keep a final *e* when adding -*ing* if:

1. The *e* follows a soft *g* and you want to keep the *j* sound. (singe + ing = *Singeing*)
2. You need to protect pronunciation (show that a preceding vowel should be long, for example, as in hoe + -ing = *hoeing*, not *hoing*).

> **3.** When an *i* precedes the final *e*, drop the *ie*, replace it with *y*, and add *-ing*. (lie + ing = *lying*)
>
> You must double the final consonant if a verb ends with a letter sequence of consonant + vowel + consonant (rub + ing = rubbing).

Rule #5: Past participle form

Add *-d* or *-ed* to regular verbs to form the past participle.

Examples:

➡ close + -d = *closed*. I had *closed* the window before it started raining.
➡ play + -ed = *played*. Terrah and I have *played* here many times before.
➡ reply + -ed = *replied*. Mrs. Jacobs had *replied* to Carly's letter in October. (In this case, the *y* is changed to an *i*.)
➡ tap + -ed = *tapped*. The spy had *tapped* out a message to his commanders before he was caught. (In this case, the *p* is doubled.)

Careful readers will notice that this form is exactly the same as the past tense form. For regular verbs, the past tense form and the past participle form will always be the same. It would be a mistake to assume that this holds true across the board, though, as we'll see when we look at irregular verbs. For now, let's practice what we've learned so far.

PRACTICE LAP

Write the correct form of each of the following verbs in the blank space.

11. I was _____ we could see each other before I left for France. (*hope*: present participle)

12. My dad _____ me off at school today. (*drop*: past tense)

13. Although I had _____ before, I wasn't very good at it. (*fish*: past participle)

14. Montgomery _____ into the front seat of the car. (*climb*: third person singular present tense)

15. What exactly are you _____? (*say*: present participle)

16. Johnson's Foods _____ our cafeteria with all their fresh vegetables. (*supply*: third person singular present tense)

17. We are _____ to leave around six o'clock in the morning. (*plan*: present participle)

18. The ferocious lion _____ on smaller animals. (*prey*: past tense)

19. I usually _____ for an hour every night. (*study*: present tense)

20. Jacqueline was _____ that she didn't bring enough water for the trip. (*concern*: past participle)

Check your answers at the end of the chapter. How did you do?

FUEL FOR THOUGHT

THE VERB *be* is a very odd duck. For starters, it is the only verb in the English language in which the infinitive differs from the present tense form of the verb. The infinitive is *to be*, while the present tense is *am, is,* or *are*. It is also, as the last sentence shows, the only verb that has a unique conjugation for use with the first person plural, second person, and third person plural. (A quick refresher: The first person singular = I *am* tired. The first person plural = We *are* tired. The second person = You or we *are* tired. The third person singular = He or she *is* tired. The third person plural = They *are* tired.)

What's more, *be* refuses to follow the rules for past tense and past participles. Every other verb has one past tense form, which is used with all subjects. Not our friend *be. Be* has two past tense forms, *was* and *were. Was* is used with first person and third person singular (I *was* tired; she *was* tired) and *were* is used with first person plural, second person, and third person plural (We *were* tired; you *were* tired; they *were* tired). The past participle of *be* is an entirely different conjugation: *been*. (I had *been* tired; they had *been* tired.)

Be is the most common verb in the English language, and misusages of the various forms of *be* are extremely common as well. All grammatically correct sentences must have subject-verb agreement, which means the subject of the sentence must be followed by the correct form of the verb. The *was/were* forms of *be* are often confused; for example, you might hear someone say something like "We *was* happy to be invited" or "They *was* still hungry after dinner." In both of these cases, the correct form of the verb is *were*.

IRREGULAR VERBS

The most common irregular verbs are listed below. Be forewarned: there are an awful lot of them, and this is not even a complete list. Do not be intimidated though; many of these verbs, you already know and use regularly. They are broken down into a few different categories to make them easier to remember.

The present participle and third person singular present tense forms are not listed for these verbs, because they follow the same rules as regular verbs.

List #1: No Change
These verbs do not change between the present tense, past tense, and past participle forms.

Present Tense	Past Tense	Past Participle
bet	bet	bet
burst	burst	burst
cost	cost	cost
cut	cut	cut

Present Tense	Past Tense	Past Participle
hit	hit	hit
hurt	hurt	hurt
let	let	let
put	put	put
quit	quit	quit
read	read	read
set	set	set
shut	shut	shut
split	split	split
spread	spread	spread

List #2: Same Past Tense and Past Participle

These verbs have the same past tense and past participle form.

Present Tense	Past Tense	Past Participle
bend	bent	bent
bleed	bled	bled
bring	brought	brought
build	built	built
buy	bought	bought
catch	caught	caught
deal	dealt	dealt
feed	fed	fed
feel	felt	felt
fight	fought	fought
find	found	found
hang	hung	hung
have	had	had
hear	heard	heard
hold	held	held
keep	kept	kept
lay	laid	laid
lead	led	led
lend	lent	lent

Present Tense	Past Tense	Past Participle
leave	left	left
lose	lost	lost
make	made	made
mean	meant	meant
meet	met	met
pay	paid	paid
plead	pled	pled
say	said	said
seek	sought	sought
sell	sold	sold
send	sent	sent
shine	shone	shone
sit	sat	sat
sleep	slept	slept
spend	spent	spent
spin	spun	spun
stand	stood	stood
strike	struck	struck
swing	swung	swung
teach	taught	taught
tell	told	told
think	thought	thought
understand	understood	understood
weep	wept	wept
win	won	won

List #3: Same Present Tense and Past Participle

These verbs have the same present tense and past participle form.

Present Tense	Past Tense	Past Participle
become	became	become
come	came	come
run	ran	run

List #4: Past Participle Ends in *-n* or *-en*

The letters *-n* and *-en* are common endings for the past participle form of irregular verbs. The most common of these verbs is listed below.

Present Tense	Past Tense	Past Participle
awake	awoke	awoken
begin	began	begun
bite	bit	bitten
blow	blew	blown
break	broke	broken
choose	chose	chosen
draw	drew	drawn
drive	drove	driven
eat	ate	eaten
fall	fell	fallen
fly	flew	flown
forbid	forbade	forbidden
forget	forgot	forgotten
forgive	forgave	forgiven
freeze	froze	frozen
get	got	gotten
give	gave	given
grow	grew	grown
hide	hid	hidden
know	knew	known
mistake	mistook	mistaken
ride	rode	ridden
rise	rose	risen
see	saw	seen
shake	shook	shaken
show	showed	shown
speak	spoke	spoken
steal	stole	stolen
take	took	taken
tear	tore	torn

Present Tense	Past Tense	Past Participle
throw	threw	thrown
wear	wore	worn
write	wrote	written

List #5: *i* becomes *a* and *u*

In some irregular verbs, the *i* in the present tense form changes to an *a* in the past tense and a *u* in the past participle.

Present Tense	Past Tense	Past Participle
drink	drank	drunk
ring	rang	rung
sing	sang	sung
sink	sank	sunk
swim	swam	swum

List #6: Options

Some irregular verbs have more than one acceptable past tense or past participle form.

Present Tense	Past Tense	Past Participle
bid	bid *or* bade	bid *or* bidden
dream	dreamed *or* dreamt	dreamed *or* dreamt
leap	leaped *or* leapt	leaped *or* leapt
prove	proved	proved *or* proven

List #7: The Rest

The following four verbs don't really follow any pattern.

Present Tense	Past Tense	Past Participle
do	did	done
go	went	gone
lie	lay	lain
light	lit	lighted

IT IS UNDERSTANDABLE that you might feel a little overwhelmed looking at these lists. There are an awful lot of irregular verbs and most of them do not seem to have any relationship to one another. You can see patterns in some words, especially rhyming words—the words *sleep, weep, sweep,* and *creep* all drop the second *e* and add a *-t* when forming their past tense and past participle (*slept, wept, swept,* and *crept*)—but these sorts of patterns usually only pertain to a handful of words. There are many words whose past tense and past participle forms end in the letters *-ought—thought, fought, bought, sought*—but a look at their present tense forms shows little connections between the verbs (*think, fight, buy, seek*).

So how are you supposed to remember all these exceptions? The best key to memorizing the irregular verbs is practice, practice, and more practice. Practice doesn't always have to be boring, however. Try to turn your practice time into a game. For instance, write the present tense forms of the irregular word list on a piece of paper. Start a timer and write down the past tense and past participle of each verb. See how long it takes you to complete the entire list and see if you can beat that time.

Sometimes it helps to practice with a friend. One game you can play is called Verb Tennis. Player one says the base form of the verb. Player two then says the past tense of the verb. Player one must then say the past participle of the verb. Player two must then respond with a new verb. The game continues until one person makes a mistake. Whoever had the last correct answer then gets a point. Play continues until one player reaches ten points.

PRACTICE LAP

Write the correct form of each of the following irregular verbs in the following blank spaces.

21. The videotape _____ that there were only two people in the room on the day of the incident. (*prove*: past tense)

22. Joaquin _____ some paper at the school store. (*buy*: past tense)

23. I am _____ the peanut butter on the bread now. (*spread*: present participle)

24. Before I knew it, I had _____ the school record. (*break*: past participle)

25. The painter _____ out the scene in pencil before he begins to paint. (*draw*: third person singular present tense)

26. Samantha is _____ lunch at the cafeteria. (*eat*: present participle)

27. Matthew _____ ready to go shopping. (*be*: past tense)

28. I had _____ my studies fall behind when I was on vacation and I had a lot to catch up on. (*let*: past participle)

29. Mrs. Collins's class _____ breakfast for the whole school this morning. (*make*: past tense)

30. I had _____ almost a whole gallon of water by the time the race started. (*drink*: past participle)

CROSSING THE FINISH LINE

In this chapter, we learned that verbs are the part of speech that expresses "existence, action, or occurrence." We learned that there are five potentially different spelling forms of verbs: present tense form, third person singular present tense form (whew!), past tense form, present participle form, and past participle form. The present tense form is also known as the base form.

We learned the following rules that apply to conjugation of regular verbs:

1. The present tense (or base) form of a verb is the infinitive of the verb minus the word *to*.
2. Add *-s* to make the third person singular present tense form. If the verb ends in a consonant + *-y* combination, change the *-y* to an *i* and add *-es*.
3. Add *-d* or *-ed* to make the past tense form.
4. Add *-ing* to form the present participle. (Don't forget the exception to this rule discussed on page 151.)
5. Add *-d* or *-ed* to regular verbs to form the past participle.

We learned that the verb *be* has several different forms, which are:

To Be	First Person Singular	Third Person Singular	First Person Plural/Second Person/Third Person Plural
present tense	am	is	are
past tense	was	was	were
present participle	being	being	being
past participle	been	been	been

We also looked at a list of irregular verbs that have to be memorized and learned a few tricks for remembering them.

GAME TIME: SPELLING SCRAMBLE

Each of the following boxes contains a scrambled word from the Chapter 8 word list with one extra letter. The number of letters in the final word is written in the parentheses next to each scrambled word. Write the unscrambled word in the blank. When you're done, you will have one letter left over. Enter these letters in order in the puzzle to find a quote from the actress Ingrid Bergman. (If you get stuck, there are clues following the scrambled word list.)

1. biclhsm (6)   __ __ __ __ __ __

2. agpionh (6)   __ __ __ __ __ __

3. ppydale (6)   — — — — — —

4. iangpys (6)   — — — — — —

5. igpdaenirs (9)   — — — — — — — — —

6. iiniievntfn (10)   — — — — — — — — — —

7. ektnae (5)   — — — — —

8. dsstuy (5)   — — — — —

9. retspens (7)   — — — — — — —

10. diperdop (7)   — — — — — — —

11. asemd (4)   — — — —

12. goedpvr (6)   — — — — — —

13. etwonad (6)   — — — — — —

14. ndruko (5)   — — — — —

15. lngdnipan (8)   — — — — — — — —

16. nhrocdeecn (9)   — — — — — — — — —

17. borenke (6)   — — — — — —

18. rtpadeip (7)   — — — — — — —

19. peticapirll (10)   — — — — — — — — — —

20. ppseusitl (8)   — — — — — — — —

21. ifdhesh (6)   — — — — — —

22. huaaedgl (7)   — — — — — — —

23. isglnimn (7)   — — — — — — —

24. gureldrrai (9)   — — — — — — — — —

25. saska (4)   — — — —

26. bubothg (6)   — — — — — —

27. padryee (6)   — — — — — —

28. nteadgi (6)   — — — — — —

29. swam (3)   — — —

30. iefx (3)   — — —

31. gmaelrur (7)   — — — — — — —

32. sopta (4)   — — — —

33. rberv (4)   — — — —

34. yelt (3)   — — —

— — — — — — —   — — —   — — — —
1   2   3   4   5   6   7   8   9   10   11   12   13   14   15

— — — — — —   — — —   —   — — —
16   17   18   19   20   21   22   23   24   25   26   27   28

— — — — — —
29   30   31   32   33   34

Spelling Scramble Clues

1. First letter: c   Last letter: s

2. First letter: h   Last letter: g

3. First letter: p   Last letter: d

4. First letter: s   Last letter: g

5. First letter: s   Last letter: g

6. First letter : i   Last letter: e

7. First letter: t   Last letter: n

8. First letter: s   Last letter: y

9. First letter: p   Last letter: t

10. First letter: d   Last letter: d

11. First letter: m   Last letter: e

12. First letter: p   Last letter: d

13. First letter: w   Last letter: d

14. First letter: d   Last letter: k

15. First letter: p   Last letter: g

16. First letter: c   Last letter: d

17. First letter: b   Last letter: n

18. First letter: t   Last letter: d

19. First letter: p   Last letter: e

20. First letter: s   Last letter: s

21. First letter: f   Last letter: d

22. First letter: l   Last letter: d

23. First letter: s   Last letter: g

24. First letter: i   Last letter: r

25. First letter: a   Last letter: s

26. First letter: b   Last letter: t

27. First letter: p   Last letter: d

28. First letter: e   Last letter: g

29. First letter: w   Last letter: s

30. First letter: f   Last letter: x

31. First letter: r   Last letter: r

32. First letter: p   Last letter: t

33. First letter: v   Last letter: b

34. First letter: l   Last letter: t

CHAPTER 8 WORD LIST

asks (ăsks)
bought (bôt)
broken (brōk´ən)
climbs (klīmz)
concerned (kŭn´sərnd)
draws (drôz)

driving (drīv´ĭng)

dropped (drŏpd)

drunk (drŭnk)

eating (ēt´ĭng)

first person (fərst pər´sən)

fished (fĭshd)

fix (fĭks)

hoping (hōp´ĭng)

infinitive (ĭn-fĭn´ə-tĭv)

irregular verb (îr´rĕg-yû-lər vŭrb)

laughed (lăft)

let (lĕt)

made (mād)

participle (pär´tə-sĭp´əl)

past participle (păst pär´tə-sĭp´əl)

past tense (păst tĕns)

planning (plăn´ĭng)

played (plād)

present participle (prĕz´ənt pär´tə-sĭp´əl)

present tense (prĕz´ənt tĕns)

preyed (prād)

proved (prüvd)

regular verb (rĕg´yû-lər vŭrb)

saying (sā´ĭng)

second person (sĕk´ənd pər´sən)

smiling (smīl´ĭng)

spreading (sprĕd´ĭng)

study (stŭd´ē-ĭng)

supplies (sŭ-plīz´)

taken (tāk´ən)

third person (thərd pər´sən)

tripped (trĭpd)

waits (wāts)

wanted (wänt´əd)

was (wŭz)

ANSWERS

1. **(1) present tense form.** The verb *fix* in this sentence refers to something that happens regularly; it is in present tense form.

2. **(3) past tense form.** The verb *wanted* tells about something that happened in the past; therefore, it is in past tense form.

3. **(5) past participle form.** You can tell that this verb is in past participle form because it uses the helping verb *have*. The *-en* ending is a common ending for irregular past participles.

4. **(2) third person singular present tense form.** The verb *asks* shows something that is happening in the present. *Jake* is a third person singular subject; therefore, this verb is in third person singular present tense form.

5. **(2) past tense form.** The verb *tripped* tells about something that happened in the past; therefore, it is in past tense form.

6. **(2) past tense form.** The verb *laughed* tells about something that happened in the past; therefore, it is in past tense form.

7. **(4) present participle form.** The *-ing* ending signifies that this verb is in present participle form.

8. **(4) present participle form.** The *-ing* ending signifies that this verb is in present participle form.

9. **(2) third person singular present tense form.** The verb *waits* shows something that happens regularly. *Virginia* is a third person singular subject; therefore, this verb is in third person singular present tense form.

10. **(5) past participle form.** You can tell that the verb *played* is in past participle form because it uses the helping verb *has*.

11. **hoping.** Add *-ing* to form the present participle of a verb (rule #4). Remember to drop the silent *e* when adding the *-ing* ending.

12. **dropped.** Add *-d* or *-ed* to verbs to form the past tense (rule #3). Remember to double the final consonant in words that end in consonant + vowel + consonant combination.

13. **fished.** Add *-d* or *-ed* to regular verbs to form the past participle. (Rule #5)

14. **climbs.** Add *-s* to make the third person singular present tense form. (Rule #2)

15. **saying.** Add *-ing* to form the present participle of a verb. (Rule #4)

16. **supplies.** Add *-s* to make the third person singular present tense form. If the verb ends in a consonant + *-y* combination, change the *-y* to an *i* and add *-es.* (Rule #2)

17. **planning.** Add *-ing* to form the present participle of a verb (rule #4). Remember to double the final consonant in words that end in a consonant + vowel + consonant combination.

18. **preyed.** Add *-d* or *-ed* to regular verbs to form the past tense. (Rule #3)

19. **study.** The present tense (or base) form of a verb is the infinitive of the verb minus the word *to.* (Rule #1)

20. **concerned.** Add *-d* or *-ed* to regular verbs to form the past participle. (Rule #5)

21. **proved.** Although the verb *prove* has an irregular past participle, the past tense is regular.

22. **bought.** The *-ought* ending is a common past tense formation, although there are few patterns that tell which verbs should end in *-ought.*

23. **spreading.** All regular and irregular verbs form their past participles by adding *-ing.*

24. **broken.** There are many irregular verbs that end in the *-en* combination.

25. **draws.** All regular and irregular verbs add *-s* to make the third person singular present tense form.

26. **eating.** All regular and irregular verbs form their present participles by adding *-ing.*

27. **was.** The verb *be* has many irregular forms.

28. **let.** The verb *let* is one of the irregular verbs that does not change in its past tense or past participle.

29. **made.** The verb *make* is an irregular verb whose forms are unique.

30. **drunk.** The verb *drink* is an irregular verb whose forms are unique.

GAME TIME: SPELLING SCRAMBLE SOLUTION

1. climbs
2. hoping
3. played
4. saying
5. spreading
6. infinitive
7. taken
8. study
9. present
10. dropped
11. made
12. proved
13. wanted
14. drunk
15. planning
16. concerned
17. broken
18. tripped
19. participle
20. supplies
21. fished
22. laughed
23. smiling
24. irregular
25. asks
26. bought
27. preyed
28. eating
29. was
30. fix
31. regular
32. past
33. verb
34. let

H	A	P	P	I	N	E	S	S		I	S		G	O	O	D
1	2	3	4	5	6	7	8	9		10	11		12	13	14	15

H	E	A	L	T	H		A	N	D		A		B	A	D
16	17	18	19	20	21		22	23	24		25		26	27	28

M	E	M	O	R	Y	.
29	30	31	32	33	34	

201 Commonly Misspelled Words

The words in this chapter are the 201 most commonly misspelled words in the English language. I've broken them down according to the traits that often cause them to be misspelled. Some of the words will have a few tricky parts, which will be identified in the notes after each section.

DOUBLE LETTERS

The following words are frequently misspelled either because they have unexpected double-letter combinations, or they do not have double-letter combinations where they would be expected. A great trick for remembering double-letter combinations is to split the pronunciation between the two letters in your head. Instead of pronouncing the word *ak-si-dent-ly*, for instance, pronounce it *ak-kid-ent-ul-lee*. This pronunciation is wrong, of course, but it's doubtful that you'll forget how to pronounce these words. Remember: There are no wrong ways to memorize spelling patterns.

accidentally	embarrass	occurrence
accommodate	fulfill	pastime
accomplish	happily	personnel
address	harass	possess
annual	immediate	questionnaire
commitment	millennium	recommend

committed	misspell	referred
committee	occasion	roommate
dissatisfied	occasionally	succeed
dumbbell	occur	until

Pay special attention to:

➡ The *acc* combination is pronounced differently in *accidentally* than in *accommodate* and *accomplish*.

➡ *Commitment* only has one *t*, while *committed* and *committee* have two *t*s. This is because final consonants are *not* doubled when the suffix begins with a consonant (*-ment*).

➡ *Dissatisfied* and *misspell* are easier to remember if you recall that the spelling of prefixes does *not* change when added to base words.

➡ *Pastime* is a compound word in which the second *t* disappears. This is a special case. *Roommate* is a compound word that behaves according to the normal rules.

➡ *Until* ends in one *l*, while *fulfill* ends in two *l*s.

C VERSUS S

The *s* and *c* sounds can cause a lot of confusion, especially when they're both found in the same word. Mnemonics can help a lot with the *s* and *c* words. For the word *absence*, for example, you could say that it's *nonsense* that the second *s* is a *c*.

absence	discipline	muscle
ascend	ecstasy	necessary
canceled	exercise	success
descend	license	
discrepancy	miscellaneous	

Pay special attention to:

➡ There is only one *l* in *canceled*.

➡ The *sc* combination in *ascend* and *descend* can be remembered because both of these words have the same root.

➡ There are two *cs* and two *ses* in *success*. There are two *ses* in *necessary*.

–ABLE VERSUS –IBLE

The suffixes *-able* and *-ible* are often pronounced the same way, making it difficult to remember which is which. When you're working to memorize these words, it helps to stress the *a* or *i* sound at the end, even if this is not how the words are really pronounced. As we learned in Chapter 3, the *-able* suffix is often added to base words that can stand alone (such as *regrettable* and *bearable*), while the *-ible* suffix is often added to roots that cannot stand alone (such as *eligible* and *susceptible*). There are exceptions to this rule, of course. The following are the most often misspelled *-able* and *-ible* words.

acceptable	eligible	manageable
accessible	feasible	noticeable
changeable	indispensable	susceptible
collectible	irresistible	usable

Pay special attention to:

➡ There are two *cs* and two *ses* in *accessible*.

➡ The *ea* combination in the word *feasible* is pronounced with a long *e* sound.

➡ *Changeable*, *manageable*, and *noticeable* all keep the silent *e* at the end of the base word for help with pronunciation. *Usable* does not.

PRACTICE LAP

There are 15 commonly misspelled words in the following paragraph. Can you spot them? Go through and circle all the misspelled words you can find.

If you have made it this far in the book, you should be very proud of your achevements. You've acomplished quite a bit already and gained valuble experiance that will undoutedly be helpful in the future. The comitment you've shown to fixing mispelled words and learning pronounciations is extrordinary. Have you been completing the exersises and gaging your performance? If you have been, then congradulations! You can allready consider yourself a sucess!

Check your answers at the end of the chapter. How did you do?

-ANCE VERSUS -ENCE AND -ANT VERSUS -ENT

As with *-able/-bile* words, the similar pronunciations of *-ance/-ence* and *-ant/-ent* cause frequent confusion. Use the trick of mispronouncing these words to remember which ending to use.

abundance	experience	permanent
acquaintance	guidance	perseverance
apparent	independence	persistence
appearance	independent	pleasant
attendance	ignorance	reference
coincidence	insurance	relevant
correspondence	intelligence	resemblance
defendant	irrelevant	sergeant
dependent	maintenance	vengeance
existence	performance	

Pay special attention to:

➡ *Acquaintance* begins with an unusual *acqu-* letter combination.
➡ The *ea* sound is different in *appearance* and *pleasant*.
➡ There is only one *r* in *apparent* and two in *correspondence*.
➡ *Defendant* is spelled with an *a*, while *dependent* is spelled with an *e*.
➡ *Resemblance* does not have an *e* between the *b* and *l*, although it is sometimes pronounced as if it does.
➡ The most common errors in this group occur with the words *independence, independent, permanent*. All three of these words have an *e* instead of an *a*.

I BEFORE *E* OR *E* BEFORE *I*?

These are the most commonly misspelled i + e combinations. Some of them, like *believe* and *medieval* follow the "*i* before *e*, except after *c*" rule, but many do not. This is a group for which there aren't too many memory tricks; sometimes, your only option is pure memorization!

achievement	height	medieval	receipt
believe	leisure	neighbor	weird
foreign	leisure	receive	

Pay special attention to:

➡ There is a silent *g* in *foreign*.
➡ *Height* and *neighbor* both have the silent *gh* combination.
➡ *Receipt* has a silent *p*.

IT'S ALL IN THE PRONUNCIATION

People sometimes have trouble with these words because they are either spelled differently than they're pronounced, or they are often mispronounced. For example, many people mistakenly say the word *across* as if it has a *t* at the end: *acrost*. Similarly, *restaurant* is usually pronounced as if the *au* in the middle was silent: *restrahnt*. For these words, it can help to carefully pronounce each sound in your head while you're spelling them.

across	congratulations	grateful	practically
again	consistent	jewelry	preferred
allege	desperate	library	privilege
always	disastrous	lightning	probably
bargain	environment	maneuver	really
basically	equipment	minuscule	recognize
biscuit	extraordinary	mischievous	restaurant
business	familiar	mysterious	schedule
candidate	February	narrator	tyranny
clothes	gauge	opportunity	undoubtedly
colonel	generally	outrageous	valuable

Pay special attention to:

➡ *Allege* and *privilege* do not have *d*s before the final *ge*.
➡ *Always* only has one *l*.
➡ *Basically*, *generally*, and *practically* end in *-ally*.
➡ The word *colonel* is pronounced *kernel*.
➡ There is no *e* in *disastrous*.
➡ *Extraordinary* is a compound word composed of *extra* and *ordinary*.
➡ The word is *undoubtedly*, not *undoubtably*.
➡ *Valuable* does not have an *e* before the *-able* suffix.

THAT DARN SCHWA

As we learned in Chapter 1, any vowel can make the schwa (ə) sound. I'm sure this gives the vowels a great feeling of togetherness, but it doesn't make it easy for the people trying to spell these words. Mnemonics can help with these words, for example: "*Calendar* has a *lend* surrounded by two *a*s."

aggravate	courtesy	parallel
analysis	definite	preparation
boundary	exhilarate	repetition
bulletin	grammar	ridiculous
calendar	humorous	separate
category	jealous	similar
courteous	murmur	

Pay special attention to:

➡ There are two *g*s in *aggravate* and two *l*s in *bulletin* and *parallel*.
➡ *Murmur* is the same three letters repeated twice.
➡ There is a silent *h* in *exhilarate*.

> ## FUEL FOR THOUGHT
>
> **ORDER! ORDER!**
>
> Waht hppanes wehn you put the ltteres of wrdos in the wonrg odrer? Can you sitll raed the snetcene? The awnesr, azmangliy, is yes! Tihs is bceusae wehn we raed, we look at the etnrie wrod, not the odrer of ecah ltteer. As lnog as the frsit and lsat ltteres are crorcet, our mndis atoumtacilaly usncarblme the rset of the ltteres in the wrod. Tihs deons't maen you sohlud go aornud pruopelsy msipsllenig wrdos, but it's a petrty cool ticrk, aynawy!

TO *E* OR NOT TO *E*

Some of these words look like they should have an extra *e* in them, but they do not. Others look like they shouldn't have an extra *e* in them, but they do.

argument	judgment	wherever
development	safety	
heroes	scary	

SILENT BUT DEADLY

The dreaded silent letters. Of course, there are many other words in the English language with silent letters, but these are the most commonly misspelled.

acquire	knowledge	subtle
column	rhyme	vacuum

Pay special attention to:

➡ *Acquire* has the same unusual *acqu-* combination as *acquaintance*.

MISSING SH OR CH

These words all sound like they should have an *sh* or *ch* sound but do not.

beneficial	conscious	negotiate
conscience	insufficient	temperature
conscientious	miniature	usually

Pay special attention to:

➡ *Conscience, conscientious,* and *conscious* all begin with the letters *consci-*.
➡ *Insufficient* does not follow the "*i* before *e*, except after *c*" rule.
➡ There is an *a* in *temperature* and two *i*'s in *miniature*.

NUMBER WORDS

When listing numbers in a series, you usually add *-th* to the original number, as with *fourth* and *thirteenth*. There are, however, some exceptions to this rule.

eighth	ninety	twelfth
fifth	ninth	

Pay special attention to:

➡ *Fifth* and *twelfth* both change their *-ve* ending to *-f*.
➡ *Ninety* keeps its silent *e*; *ninth* does not.

JUST PLAIN WEIRD

These words don't follow a common pattern; they just have to be memorized.

already	fiery	precede	warranty
all right	guarantee	pronunciation	
cemetery	imaginary	rhythm	
exceed	length	supersede	

Pay special attention to:

➡ *Already* is one word with only one *l*. *All right* is two words. *Alright* is sometimes used when writing dialogue, but the correct spelling is *all right*.

➡ The suffixes of *cemetery* and *imaginary* have the same pronunciation.

➡ *Exceed*, *precede*, and *supersede* have the same root spelled three different ways.

➡ The adjective meaning "full of fire" is spelled *fiery*, not *firey*.

➡ *Guarantee* and *warranty* are synonyms that sound similar but have completely different spellings.

➡ *Pronunciation* is derived from the word *pronounce*. Note that *pronunciation* does not have an *o* between the *n* and the *u*.

PRACTICE LAP

Circle the correct spelling of the following words.

1. muscle   mussle

2. correspondance   correspondence

3. scarey   scary

4. alledge   allege

5. column   collum

6. milennium   millennium

7. forfeit   forfiet

8. feasable   feasible

9. twelfth   twelth

10.	narrarator	narrator
11.	supersede	supercede
12.	useable	usable
13.	occassion	occasion
14.	miniature	miniture
15	separate	seperate

Check your answers at the end of the chapter. How did you do?

CROSSING THE FINISH LINE

In this chapter, we looked at the 201 most commonly misspelled words in the English language and learned some tips for remembering them.

GAME TIME: RIDDLE ME THIS

In each of the following sentences, circle the correctly spelled version of the italicized word. Then, write that word in the corresponding box on page 182. When you're done, enter the letters in the shaded boxes into the blanks following the puzzle to find the answer to the riddle.

1. "What seems to be the (*occasion/ocassion*)?" asked Mr. Winslow.

2. McCarthy was at the (*hiegte/height*) of his powers in 1950.

3. The clock was no longer (*useble/usable*) after its hands snapped off.

4. It was (*apparent/apaarent*) that the traffic was going to be bad.

5. My (*nouledge/knowledge*) of history does not extend much farther back than the medieval period.

6. I find the aroma of blueberry pie to be (*irrersistible/irrestable*).

7. The country was worried that the computer virus would spread at the (*millennium/milleenium*).

8. Tito won't be able to (*fulfill/fullfil*) his obligation tonight.

9. We'll need (*perseverance/persaverence*) to climb the mountain before nightfall.

10. We might need to take Buffy to (*dicsipline/discipline*) school.

11. Baseball is the American (*pastime/passtim*).

12. The judge demanded an (*independant/independent*) investigation.

13. My mother told me to (*address/adress*) the envelope to Mrs. Porochista.

14. Please get a (*receite/receipt*) for breakfast.

15. Would you like a (*bisckit/biscuit*) with your dinner?

16. In my (*judgment/jugement*), Ricardo should pay for the broken window.

17. Check the (*schedule/schejule*) and see what time the movie starts.

18. Little children are more (*susseptable/susceptible*) to most diseases than adults.

19. Put the numbers in a (*columm/column*) before adding them.

20. The spy gathered important (*intelligence/intellijence*) for his government.

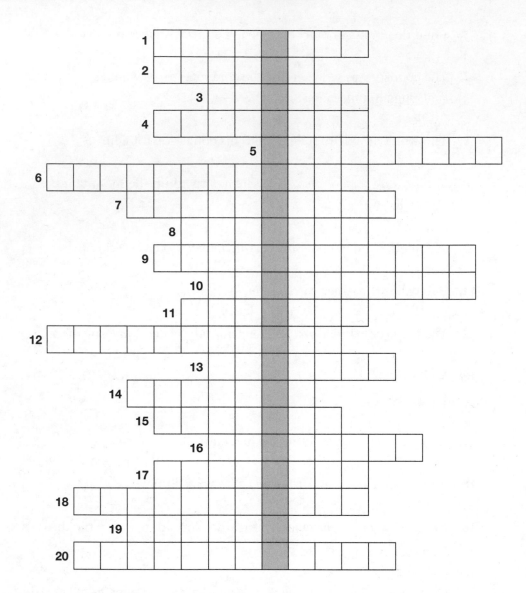

Riddle: What is a dessert that bites?

Answer: __ __ __ __ __ – __ __ __ __ __ __ __ __

__ __ __ __ __ __ __.

CHAPTER 9 WORD LIST

absence (ăb´səns)
abundance (ə-bŭnd´əns)

acceptable (ăk-sĕpt´ə-bəl)

accessible (ăk-sĕs´ə-bəl)

accidentally (ăk-sĭd-ĕnt´lē)

accommodate (ə-kŏm´ə-dāt)

accomplish (ə-kŏm´plĭsh)

achievement (ə-chēv´mənt)

acquaintance (ə-kwānt´əns)

acquire (ə-kwī´ər)

across (ə-krŏs´)

address (ăd´drĕs)

again (ə-gĕn´)

aggravate (ăg´rə-vāt)

all right (ôl rīt)

allege (ə-lĕj´)

already (ŏl-rĕd´ē)

always (ôl´wāz)

analysis (ə-năl´ə-sĭs)

annual (ăn´yû-əl)

apparent (ə-pâr´ənt)

appearance (ə-pîr´əns)

argument (ärg´yû-mənt)

ascend (ə-sĕnd´)

attendance (ə-tĕn´dəns)

bargain (bär´gən)

basically (bās´ĭk-lē)

believe (bē-lēv´)

beneficial (bĕn-ə-fĭsh´əl)

biscuit (bĭs´kət)

boundary (bownd´ər-ē)

bulletin (bŭl´ə-tĭn)

business (bĭz´nəs)

calendar (kăl´ən-dər)

canceled (kăn´səld)

candidate (kăn´də-dāt)

category (kăt´ə-gōr-ē)

cemetery (sĕm´ə-tār-ē)

changeable (chănj´ə-bəl)

clothes (klō*thz*)

coincidence (kō-ĭn′sə-dəns)

collectible (kəl-ĕkt′ə-bəl

colonel (kər′nəl)

column (kŏl′əm)

commitment (kəm-mĭt′mənt)

committed (kəm-mĭt′əd)

committee (kəm-mĭt′ē)

congratulations (kən-graj-yû′lā-shənz)

conscience (kŏn′shəns)

conscientious (kŏn-shē-ĕn′shəs)

conscious (kŏn′shəs)

consistent (kən-sĭs′tənt)

correspondence (kōr-ə-spŏnd′əns)

courteous (kər′tē-əs)

courtesy (kər′tə-sē)

defendant (dē-fĕnd′ənt)

definite (dĕf′ĭn-ĭt)

dependent (dē-pĕnd′ənt)

descend (dē-sĕnd′)

desperate (dĕs′pər-ət)

development (dē-vĕl′əp-mənt)

disastrous (dĭs-ăst′rəs)

discipline (dĭs′ə-plĭn)

discrepancy (dĭs-krĕp′ən-sē)

dissatisfied (dĭs-săt′ĭs-fīd)

dumbbell (dŭm′bĕl)

ecstasy (ĕk′stə-sē)

eighth (āth)

eligible (ĕl′ĭj-ə-bəl)

embarrass (əm-bār-əs)

environment (ən-vī′ərn-mənt)

equipment (ē-kwĭp′mənt)

exceed (ĕk-sēd′)

exercise (ĕk′sər-sīz)

exhilarate (ĕk-zĭl′ər-āt)

existence (ĕk-zĭs´təns)

experience (ĕk-pîr´ē-əns)

extraordinary (ĕk-strôrd´ĭn-ār-ē)

familiar (fəm-ĭl´yər)

feasible (fēz´ə-bəl)

February (fĕb´yû-ār-ē)

fiery (fī´ər-ē)

fifth (fĭfth)

foreign (fōr´ən)

forfeit (fōr´fĭt)

fulfill (fŭl´fĭl)

gauge (gāj)

generally (jĕn´rə-lē)

grammar (grăm-ər)

grateful (grāt´fəl)

guarantee (gâr´ən-tē)

guidance (gīd´əns)

happily (hăp´ə-lē)

harass (hə´răs)

height (hīt)

heroes (hēr´ōz)

humorous (hyû´mər-əs)

ignorance (ĭg´nər-əns)

imaginary (ĭm-ăj´ĭn-âr-ē)

immediate (ĭm-ēd´ē-ət)

independence (ĭn-də-pĕnd´əns)

independent (ĭn-də-pĕnd´ənt)

indispensable (ĭn-dĭs-pĕns´ə-bəl)

insufficient (ĭn-sŭ-fĭsh´ənt)

insurance (ĭn-shər´əns)

intelligence (ĭn-tĕl´ə-gəns)

irrelevant (îr-rĕl´ə-vənt)

irresistible (îr-rə-sĭst´ə-bəl)

jealous (jĕl´əs)

jewelry (jü´əl-rē)

judgment (jŭj´mənt)

knowledge (nŏl´əj)

leisure (lē´shər)

length (lĕngth)

library (lī´brăr-ē)

license (lī´səns)

lightning (līt´nĭng)

maintenance (mān´tən-əns)

manageable (măn´ə-jə-bəl)

maneuver (mən-ü´vər)

medieval (məd-ē-vəl)

millennium (məl-ĕn´ē-əm)

miniature (mĭn´ĭ-chyûr)

minuscule (mĭn´ĭ-skyûl)

miscellaneous (mĭs-səl-ān´ē-əs)

mischievous (mĭs´chə-vəs)

misspell (mĭs-spĕl´)

murmur (mŭr´mər)

muscle (mŭ´səl)

mysterious (mĭst-îr´ē-əs)

narrator (nâr´ā-tər)

necessary (nĕs´ə-sār-ē)

negotiate (nə-gō´shē-āt)

neighbor (nā´bər)

ninety (nīn´tē)

ninth (nīnth)

noticeable (nō´tĭs-ə-bəl)

occasion (ō-kā´zhən)

occasionally (ō-kā´zhən-əl-ē)

occur (ə-kər´)

occurrence (ə-kər´əns)

opportunity (ôp-ər-tün´ĭ-tē)

outrageous (owt-rāj´əs)

parallel (pâr´əl-ĕl)

pastime (păst´īm)

performance (pər-fôrm´əns)

permanent (pər´mən-ənt)

perseverance (pər-sə-vîr´əns)

persistence (pər-sĭst´əns)

personnel (pər-sən-ĕl´)

pleasant (plĕz´ənt)

possess (pə-zĕs´)

practically (prăk´tĭk-lē)

precede (prə-sēd´)

preferred (prə-fərd´)

preparation (prĕp-ər-ā´shən)

privilege (prĭv´ləj)

probably (prŏb´əb-lē)

pronunciation (prō-nŭn-sĭ-ā´shən)

questionnaire (kwĕs-chən-âr´)

really (rĭl´ē)

receipt (rə-sēt´)

receive (rə-sēv´)

recognize (rĕk´əg-nīz)

recommend (rĕk-ə-mĕnd´)

reference (rĕf´rəns)

referred (rē-fərd´)

relevant (rĕl´ə-vənt)

repetition (rĕp-ə-tĭsh´ən)

resemblance (rē-zĕm´bləns)

restaurant (rĕs´trônt)

rhyme (rīm)

rhythm (rĭ-*th*əm)

ridiculous (rē-dĭk´yû-ləs)

roommate (rüm´āt)

safety (sāf´tē)

scary (skăr´ē)

schedule (skĕd´yû-əl)

separate (sĕp´ər-āt)

sergeant (sâr´jənt)

similar (sĭm´ə-lər)

subtle (sŭ´təl)

succeed (sŭk-sēd´)

success (sŭk-sĕs´)

supersede (sü-pər-sēd´)

susceptible (sŭ-sĕpt´ə-bəl)

temperature (tĕmp´ər-chər)

twelfth (twĕlfth)

tyranny (tîr´ə-nē)

undoubtedly (ŭn-dowt´əd-lē)

until (ŭn-tĭl´)

usable (yûz´ə-bəl)

usually (yû´zhəl-lē)

vacuum (văk´yûm)

valuable (văl´yû-bəl)

vengeance (vĕn´jəns)

warranty (wôr-ən-tē)

weird (wîrd)

wherever (whâr-ĕv´ər)

ANSWERS

15 Misspelled Words

If you have made it this far in the book, you should be very proud of your **achevements**. You've **acomplished** quite a bit already and gained **valuble experiance** that will **undoutedly** be helpful in the future. The **comitment** you've shown to fixing **mispelled** words and learning **pronounciations** is **extrordinary**. Have you been completing the **exersises** and **gaging** your **performence**? If you have been, then **congradulations**! You can **allready** consider yourself a **sucess**!

1. **muscle.** Remember that *muscle* has an *s* + *c* combination in the middle.
2. **correspondence.** Don't forget the double *rs* and *-ence* ending on *correspondence*.
3. **scary.** *Scary* changes the silent *e* of *scare* to a *y*.
4. **allege.** Remember that there is no *d* in *allege*.
5. **column.** The silent *n* is the trickiest part of the word *column*.

6. **millennium.** Remember the two *ls* and two *ns* in *millennium*.

7. **forfeit.** *Forfeit* does not abide by the "*i* before *e*, except after *c*" rule.

8. **feasible.** Remember that the suffix on *feasible* is *-ible*, not *-able*.

9. **twelfth.** *Twelfth*, *fifth*, and *eighth* are the three sequence words that do not follow regular spelling rules.

10. **narrator.** Some people pronounce the word *narrarator*, but there is no second *ar* combination in the word.

11. **supersede.** The endings of *supersede*, *exceed*, and *recede* are easily confused.

12. **usable.** The word *use* drops the silent *e* when adding the suffix *-able*.

13. **occasion.** Don't forget the double-*c* combination in *occasion*.

14. **miniature.** The *a* in *miniature* isn't always pronounced, but it still belongs there.

15. **separate.** This word is often misspelled *seperate*; just pronounce it *sep-AR-ate* in your head and you should remember the correct spelling.

Game Time: Riddle Me This Solution

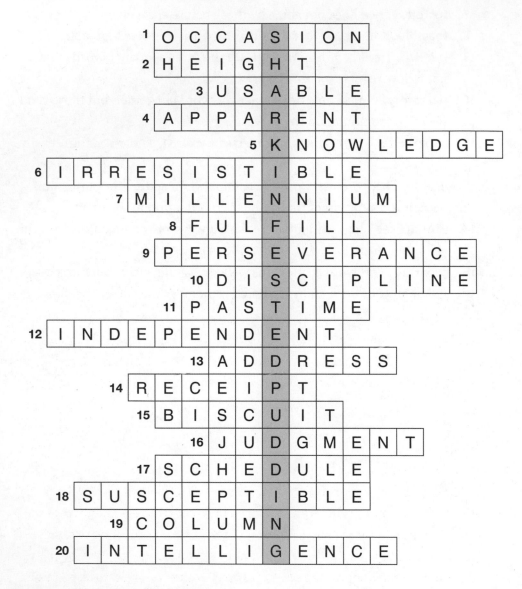

1. OCCASION
2. HEIGHT
3. USABLE
4. APPARENT
5. KNOWLEDGE
6. IRRESISTIBLE
7. MILLENNIUM
8. FULFILL
9. PERSEVERANCE
10. DISCIPLINE
11. PASTIME
12. INDEPENDENT
13. ADDRESS
14. RECEIPT
15. BISCUIT
16. JUDGMENT
17. SCHEDULE
18. SUSCEPTIBLE
19. COLUMN
20. INTELLIGENCE

Riddle: What is a dessert that bites?

Answer: Shark-infested pudding.

The Living Language

As you learned in Chapter 3, a large percentage of English roots come from Latin. Latin forms the basis of many of the languages spoken in the Americas and Europe, a group of languages that is collectively known as the **Romance** languages. The Romance languages include Spanish, Portuguese, French, Italian, Romanian, and Catalan, a language spoken in a small European country called Andorra and parts of Spain and Italy. Although many of our words are derived from Latin, English is officially considered **a Germanic** language because of its grammatical structure. Still, if you've ever taken Spanish, French, or Italian, you know that Romance and Germanic languages share a lot of similarities.

Most people stopped speaking Latin regularly around the 1600s. It is still studied by many scholars and spoken in select circles—members of the Catholic Church, for instance, often use Latin in ceremonies and readings—but it is not the primary means of communication for any country or group of people on earth. For this reason, it is sometimes referred to as a "dead" language.

By contrast, English is very much alive. In 2007 alone, more than 100 new words and phrases were added to the Merriam-Webster Collegiate dictionary, including *smackdown* (the act of bringing down an opponent) and *ginormous* (ridiculously huge). In this chapter, we'll be taking a look at words that have come into English from a variety of sources, including foreign words, old words that are being used in new ways, and brand-new words that are just joining the language.

PRACTICE LAP

In the following exercises, choose the word or term that correctly fits the definition.

1. noun: money due to a person or business
   a. insurance
   b. network
   c. product
   d. credit

2. noun: the crucial moment in a story
   a. climax
   b. anecdote
   c. vegan
   d. archetype

3. adjective: involving the common people
   a. globalization
   b. grassroots
   c. online
   d. viral

4. adjective or adverb: with one's identity concealed
   a. anecdote
   b. incognito
   c. naïve
   d. implement

5. adjective: computer software or hardware that easily is used by someone with limited knowledge
   a. keyword
   b. user-friendly
   c. résumé
   d. compatible

6. noun: the specialized vocabulary of an industry or group
   a. jargon
   b. policy
   c. keywords
   d. corporation

7. verb: the process of entering information into a computer
   a. interview
   b. downloading
   c. rhetoric
   d. input

8. noun: the course of events in a story
   a. theme
   b. tone
   c. plot
   d. setting

9. noun: the program a user uses to look at files on the Web
   a. browser
   b. network
   c. search engine
   d. upload

10. noun: a phrase or saying that has been overused and, as a result, has little significance
    a. spiel
    b. satire
    c. pun
    d. cliché

Check your answers at the end of the chapter. How did you do?

FOREIGN WORDS

Although all English words were originally derived from other sources, certain words have been adopted into the English language directly from other languages without any changes. Often, we have taken these words because there are no English words that carry the same meaning. Other foreign words are used in writing about history or politics. Twenty commonly used foreign words and terms are defined below.

aficionado (ə-fish-ē-ə-nä'dō) *n.* a person who likes, knows about, and is devoted to a particular activity or thing. *Jonelle has been a baseball aficionado ever since she went to her first game with her dad.*

amigo (ə-mē'gō) *n.* friend. *My amigo Carl goes to school on the other side of town.*

blasé (blä-zā') *adj.* boring as a result of overexposure. *This movie seemed exciting at first, but it became blasé after the third car chase.*

bravo (brä-vō') *int.* great job. *Bravo! Well done!*

bourgeois (bôr-zwä') *adj.* showing excessive concern for materialistic goods. *Pete's bourgeois values leave him always wanting more.*

cliché (klē-shā') *n.* a phrase or saying that has been overused and, as a result, has little significance. *The lyrics to this song are full of meaningless clichés.*

connoisseur (kŏn-nō-sür') *n.* one who knows a lot about a certain subject. *Fernando is a connoisseur of cheese.*

coup de grâce (kü də grâs') *n.* the final triumph. *The Pistons' final coup de grâce was a game-ending fourth-quarter dunk.*

debut (dā-byû') *n.* a first appearance. *The tennis player was nervous about her professional debut.*

déjà vu (dā-zhä vü') *n.* the feeling that one has been in a situation before. *I had a sensation of déjà vu when I saw my younger sister wearing my old jacket.*

entrepreneur (ŏn-trə-prə-nü'ər) *n.* a person who starts his or her own business. *Being an entrepreneur can be risky because you never know if you will be successful.*

facade (fə-säd') *n.* a false front. *I thought John had gotten over his dog's death, but I learned later his happy face was just a facade.*

incognito (ĭn-kŏg-nē'tō) *adj.* or *adv.* with one's identity concealed. *The singer didn't want to be recognized at the restaurant so she went incognito.*

laissez-faire (lĕs-zā fâr') *n.* a policy opposing government control of economic matters except in the case of maintaining peace and the concept of property. *He believed in a laissez-faire system in which he was free to spend his money on anything he wanted.*

malaise (məl-āz') *n.* a feeling of mental unease or discomfort. *There was a general malaise at the school after our baseball team lost the playoffs.*

naïve (nī-ēv') *adj.* innocent, simple, lacking knowledge of the world. *I told him he was naïve to think that he could pass the test without studying.*

non sequitur (nŏn sĕ'kwĭt-ər) *n.* a statement that has no connection to the previous statement or idea. *The politician started out talking about the homeless problem, then launched into a non sequitur about his vacation in Alaska.*

passé (pă-sā') *adj.* out of fashion. *Tight jeans are so passé this year.*

rendezvous (rŏn'dā-vü) *n.* meeting or *v.* to meet. *We decided to rendezvous at the swing set during lunch.*

spiel (shpēl) *n.* talk given for the purpose of luring an audience or selling a product. *The salesman's spiel made the vacuum cleaner seem more impressive than it really was.*

vendetta (vĕn-dĕt'ə) *n.* a grudge or feud characterized by acts of retaliation. The Count of Monte Cristo *is a classic adventure story about a falsely imprisoned man who carries out a vendetta against his captors.*

FUEL FOR THOUGHT

BY THE YEAR 2050, it is estimated that 30% of the United States population will be descended from families with roots in Spanish-speaking countries. For people who study languages, the rise of the Hispanic and Latino populations offers a unique opportunity to explore what happens when two different languages come together. In many communities around the country, a mixture of Spanish and English known as **Spanglish** is becoming increasingly common.

Spanglish is not recognized as an official language in the way that Spanish and English are. It is a combination of Spanish and English by people who speak both languages fluently and are able to switch between them effortlessly. A typical Spanglish sentence might begin in English, switch to Spanish in the middle, and end back in English. It is often spoken by second-generation immigrants (the children of people who moved to the United States from Spanish-speaking countries) who are used to speaking one language at home and another language at school.

No one knows whether Spanglish will develop into its own language or if it will fade away in future generations. Although it may not exist in the same form as it does today, there is no doubt that the combination of English and Spanish will continue to have an important effect on the language we speak.

LITERARY WORDS

Literary words are words that are useful when discussing or analyzing a piece of literature such as a novel, short story, or poem. Some of these words are only applicable to literature; others can also be used to describe real-world situations.

anecdote (ăn′ĭk-dōt) *n.* a short account of an interesting or humorous incident. *Our teacher told us a comical anecdote about her college days.*

archetype (är′kĭ-tīp) *n.* an original model or type after which other similar things are patterned. *Shakespeare's* Romeo and Juliet *is the archetype of the tragic love story.*

climax (klī′măks) *n.* the crucial moment in a story. *The criminal was caught at the climax of the story.*

exposition (ĕks-pō-zĭsh-ən) *n.* the part of the story that sets up the plot. *Important details about the story were revealed during the exposition.*

figurative (fĭg′ûr-ə-tĭv) *adj.* not literal. *Writers often use figurative language when writing about nature.*

hyperbole (hī-pər´bŭ-lē) *n.* intentional exaggeration. *It is hyperbole to say that you are dying of thirst when you're just a little thirsty.*

interpret (ĭn-tər´prĭt) *v.* to explain the meaning of. *I don't know how to interpret the doctor's writing.*

irony (ī´rŭn-ē) *n.* the use of words to express something different from the literal meaning. *The irony of his nickname, "Tiny," became obvious when I discovered he was seven-feet tall.*

literal (lĭt´ər-əl) *adj.* the actual meaning. *The literal translation of his name means "king."*

personification (pər-sŏn´ĭ-fĭ-kā-shən) *n.* the act of giving an inanimate object or animal humanlike properties. *Calling the sea "angry" is an example of personification.*

plot (plŏt) *n.* the course of events in a story. *The plot of this story is exciting and action-packed.*

protagonist (prō-tăg´ə-nĭst) *n.* the main character in a story. *The protagonist of the story is a young wizard named Harry.*

pun (pŭn) *n.* play on words. *The title of the vampire movie* Love at First Bite *was a pun on the saying "love at first sight."*

rhetoric (rĕ´tōr-ĭk) *n.* style of speaking. *I decided to vote for the politician when I heard his fiery and convincing rhetoric.*

satire (să´tī-ər) *n.* a literary style in which important topics are made to look ridiculous through the use of humor. *The movie* Network *is a classic satire on media.*

setting (sĕt´ĭng) *n.* the environment or location in which a story takes place. *The setting of* Catcher in the Rye *is New York City.*

stanza (stănz´ə) *n.* a group of lines in a poem. *This poem is composed of three stanzas.*

summarize (sŭm´ər-īz) *v.* to highlight the most important details. *Our teacher asked us to summarize our summer vacations.*

theme (thēm) *n.* the main idea of a story. *The theme of this book is "never give up."*

tone (tōn) *n.* the feeling of a story. *This scene of the play has a foreboding tone.*

BUSINESS WORDS

Business words are words that relate to work or finances. You may see these words used in newspapers and magazine articles. Although they may not mean much to you right now, someday you will probably use most of these words on a regular basis.

balance (băl'əns) *n.* the difference between money available and money owed. *After I pay for my new shoes, the balance on my account will be $500.*
bankrupt (băngk'rŭpt) *n.* the legal state of being unable to pay ones debts. *Mr. Temple's company went bankrupt when demand for their product died out.*
benefits (bĕn'ə-fĭtz) *n.* anything offered by an employer in addition to salary, including health insurance, vacation days, and sick days. *My job doesn't pay very well but the benefits are excellent.*
corporation (kôr-pôr-ā'shŭn) *n.* a company that is legally treated as an individual. *Wal-Mart is one of the most successful corporations in the world.*
credit (krĕd'ĭt) *n.* money due to a person or business. *I have a credit of $25 at the bookstore that I can spend on whatever I would like.*
debt (dĕt) *n.* money owed by a person or business. *My debt is low because I always pay with cash.*
department (dē-pärt'mĕnt) *n.* a smaller division within a company. *The accounting department handles all of our financial transactions.*
employer (ĕm-ploi'ər) *n.* business or individual for whom an employee works. *My employer has a great health insurance plan.*
fiscal (fĭs'kəl) *adj.* financial. *My dad loves to talk about fiscal responsibility.*
implement (ĭm'plĭ-mĕnt) *v.* to put into effect. *The company decided to implement some changes to its e-mail policy.*
insurance (ĭn-shyûr'ĕns) *n.* a coverage plan in which an individual pays a regular fee in exchange for future services. *According to our health insurance plan, we are allowed two dentist visits every year.*
incur (ĭn'kər) *v.* to come into or acquire, usually undesirably. *We have incurred a large number of debts.*
interview (ĭn'tər-vyû) *n.* a formal meeting set up between an employer and employee when attempting to be hired for a job. *I have an interview with the cement factory on Monday.*

jargon (jär´gən) *n.* the specialized vocabulary of an industry or group. *Once I learned all the jargon, my job as a computer engineer became much easier.*

policy (pŏl-ə´sē) *n.* a course of action; a rule. *Our policy is to treat everyone equally.*

procedure (prō-cē´jyûr) *n.* a way of doing something. *The procedure is to always wash your hands before cooking food.*

product (prŏ´dŭkt) *n.* a thing being produced or manufactured. *The company's new product is expected to sell well.*

references (rĕf´rən-sĭz) *n.* a group of people presented by a potential employee to an employer who can report on the potential employee's strengths and weaknesses. *I have great references from my years spent working for the Parks Department.*

résumé (rĕ´zə–mā) *n.* a printed overview of one's previous job experience. *As Omar's résumé shows, he has a long history of working with web-based companies.*

salary (săl´ə-rē) *n.* the amount a job pays, usually figured as an annual amount. *My annual salary is $45,000.*

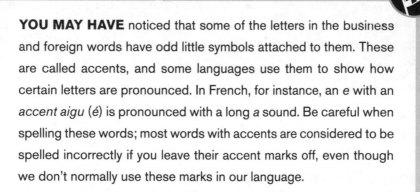

CAUTION!

YOU MAY HAVE noticed that some of the letters in the business and foreign words have odd little symbols attached to them. These are called accents, and some languages use them to show how certain letters are pronounced. In French, for instance, an *e* with an *accent aigu* (*é*) is pronounced with a long *a* sound. Be careful when spelling these words; most words with accents are considered to be spelled incorrectly if you leave their accent marks off, even though we don't normally use these marks in our language.

TECHNOLOGY WORDS

The interesting thing about technology terms is that the definition of technology itself is constantly changing. Technically (no pun intended), technology refers to any sort of man-made machine. A wheelbarrow, for example, is a form of technology. However, if someone tells you they're really into technology, it's a pretty good guess that they don't mean they're really into wheelbarrows. More often than not, technology refers to modern electronics and computer terms. Here, then, are 20 computer and electronics terms that are useful in the modern world.

application (ăp-lĭ-kā′shŭn) *n.* a software program that lets you complete a task on your computer, such as word processing, listening to music, or viewing a web page. *The computer application I use for making spreadsheets has many other uses.*

bandwidth (bănd′wĭth) *n.* the capacity for sending information through an Internet connection. *I have a lot of bandwidth at work, which makes it easy to download large files.*

browser (brow′zər) *n.* the program that enables users to look at files on the Web. *My favorite browser is Firefox.*

cursor (kər′sər) *n.* a symbol, usually a blinking line or arrow, that shows the location of an input device on the screen. *Point your cursor at the button reading submit and click the left mouse button.*

database (dā′tə-bās) *n.* an organizational system using tables that helps a computer quickly retrieve pieces of information. *The names of all the DVDs this store offers are collected in a database.*

digital (dĭ-jĭ-təl) *adj.* the description of any electronic device that uses numbers to calculate information. *This digital thermometer beeps when your temperature has been attained.*

download (down′lōd) *v.* the process of copying files from an outside source to your computer or network location. *My favorite band is offering a deal where fans can download their latest song.*

gigabyte (gĭg′ə-bīt) or **gig** (gĭg) *n.* a measure of storage capacity equal to one billion bytes; currently the predominant measure of hard drive space. *Benton bought a new computer with a 750-gig hard drive.*

hard drive (hârd´ drīv) *n.* the part of a computer on which information is stored. *I had to buy a new hard drive because I couldn't get access to any of my files.*

input (ĭn´pŏŏt) *v.* the process of entering information into a computer. *After you input the requested information, the computer will give you your new password.*

keyword (kē´wərd) *n.* a word connected to a larger concept used to simplify web searches. *If you want to find information about the Civil War, type the keywords* U.S. *and* Civil War *into a search engine.*

login (log´ĭn) *n.* the process of identifying oneself to a computer or network location, usually by entering a username and password. *Here is your new login information; keep it in a safe place.*

mouse (mows) *n.* a sliding input device with one or two buttons used to operate a cursor on a computer screen. *With my wireless mouse, I can surf the Web from across the room.*

network (nĕt´wərk) *n.* a group of two or more computers linked together. *More than 200 computers are connected by the school network.*

online (ŏn´līn) *adj.* connected to a computer or network. *Online shopping now accounts for the majority of all money spent in the United States.*

search engine (sərch´ ĭn-jĭn) *n.* a program that searches documents, websites, and databases by keywords and returns a list of related information. *Yahoo! used to be the leading search engine, until it was overtaken by Google.*

spreadsheet (sprĕd´shēt) *n.* a bookkeeping program that displays data in rows and columns, or any individual document created by that program. *I have the names of all of my CDs arranged on a spreadsheet.*

text (tĕkst) *v.* to send a message by text message, usually on a cell phone. *Text me the time the movie starts and I'll meet you there.*

upload (ŭp´lōd) *v.* the process of copying to from an outside source from your computer or network location. *When you're done with your test, upload your answers to the server to see the results.*

username (yû´zər-nām) *n.* a nickname used to log on to a computer, website, or network location. *The username I use to get onto my family's computer is "nexxus."*

BUZZWORDS

If something has "buzz," it means that a lot of people are talking about it. A movie with good buzz is a movie that a lot of people enjoy. A buzzword, on the other hand, is a new word that suddenly leaps into popular usage. Interestingly, the term buzz started life as a buzzword itself, having originally been used by advertisers to describe the beelike excitement generated by a popular fad or product. Often, buzzwords are related to technology or business. They either get adopted into the language as regular vocabulary or quickly die from overuse . . . so use these words as much as you can right now, before they disappear!

blog (blôg) *n.* or *v.* short for "weblog," an online diary or collection of frequently updated information; or the process of updating that information. *I read all about your Thanksgiving dinner on your blog.*

blogosphere (blôg´ō-sfîr) *n.* a collective term for the community of weblogs and bloggers. *The blogosphere can't stop talking about the latest celebrity scandal.*

branding (brănd´ĭng) *n.* a marketing term, the definition of a company for advertising purposes. *The local grocery chain is in the process of updating its branding to seem more modern.*

compatible (kŭm-păt´ĭbəl) *adj.* able to work together, often used to describe software or computer devices. *Is this monitor compatible with my operating system?*

content (kŏn´tĕnt) *n.* substantive information. *I enjoy this website because it always has new content.*

diversity (dī-vər´sĭ-tē) *n.* a state consisting of a variety of different elements; often used in referring to race or ethnicity. *My new employer encourages diversity in the workplace.*

globalization (glō-bəl-ĭ-zā´shən) *n.* the state of extending to all parts of the globe, often used in reference to economic matters. *Some people believe that the globalization of companies and services is bad for local culture.*

grassroots (grăs-rüts´) *adj.* involving the common people. *The presidential campaign is a grassroots effort.*

green (grēn) *adj.* environmentally friendly. Green building materials are all the rage right now.

newbie (nü´bē) *n.* someone who is doing something for the first time. *I have to help Marcus out with his online profile because he's a newbie.*

outsource (owt´sôrs) *v.* to contract jobs to outside workers. *The automobile manufacturer outsources much of its work to China.*

social networking (sō´shəl nĕt´wərk-ĭng) *v.* the use of a website to connect with people who share common interests or qualities. *MySpace is one of the most popular sites for social networking.*

sustainable (sŭs-tān´ə-bəl) *adj.* capable of being continued with minimal long-term environmental effects. *Transportation is becoming more sustainable with the invention of such devices as the hybrid engine.*

sticky (stĭk´ē) *adj.* attracting viewers or readers. *We have to create a sticky website that people will want to return to often.*

tipping point (tĭp´ĭng point) *n.* the moment from which there is no return. *Our country is nearing a tipping point in the availability of oil.*

transparent (trăns-pâr´ĕnt) *adj.* open about operating procedures. *The government is taking steps to become more transparent to enhance their trustworthiness among average citizens.*

user-friendly (yû´zər frĕnd´lē) *adj.* computer software or hardware that easily used by someone with limited knowledge. *This website gets more hits than other, similar websites because it is more user-friendly.*

vegan (vē´gən) *n.* or *adj.* someone who does not eat any animal-derived foods or use any animal byproducts; description of a food item or product containing no animal-derived ingredients or byproducts. *Sarah became a vegan after learning more about how meat is processed.*

viral (vī´rəl) *adj.* an online phenomenon that duplicates like a virus, getting passed around between through e-mail or word-of-mouth. *Five different people sent me the latest viral video.*

virtual (vər´chü´əl) *adj.* carried on through a computer. *Our class held a virtual discussion today in a chat room.*

INSIDE TRACK

MANY OF THE words in this chapter are more difficult than the words we've studied in previous chapters. However, if you've been following the book closely and doing the exercises, the knowledge you've gained can be put to use in remembering how to spell words of any length or difficulty.

Take a word like *globalization*, for instance. Upon first sight, it might appear to be a difficult word to remember. But look closely at its parts. Start by breaking the word down into syllables, as you learned in Chapter 3: *glob-al-iz-a-tion*. You know that this word is related to the earth, and the earth is a globe, so you can guess that the base word of *globalization* is *globe*. The other parts of the word are all suffixes: *-al*, *-ize*, *-ation*. Chapter 6 taught you the spelling rules of adding suffixes; in this case, you have to drop the silent *e* on the end of *globe* and *-ize*. Put all of the parts together, and you get *globalization*.

PRACTICE LAP

Circle the word or term that is spelled correctly in each of the following groups.

11. passay   passé

12. backrupt   bankrupt

13. debt   det

14. anekdote   anecdote

15. spreadsheet   spreadshete

16. stanza   stonza

17.	contint		content
18.	users name		username
19.	brooser		browser
20.	naivë		naïve
21.	compatible		commpattible
22.	sustainible		sustainable
23.	fiscal		fiscul
24.	hyperbole		hyperbowl
25.	entrapruner		entrepreneur

Check your answers at the end of the chapter. How did you do?

CROSSING THE FINISH LINE

In this chapter, we looked at five different categories of words that are useful to know: foreign words, literary words, business words, technology words, and buzzwords.

GAME TIME: SEARCH-A-WORD

The following sentences contain 32 misspelled words from the Chapter 10 word list. First, determine which words are spelled incorrectly, and write the correct versions in the blanks following the sentences. Then, find and circle these words in the puzzle. The words can be found vertically, horizontally, diagonally, backward, or forward. Happy hunting! (Note: Accent marks and hyphens are omitted from the Search-A-Word puzzle.)

1. Even though my amego Mark is a film afficionado, he still didn't understand the clymax to the movie.

2. Could you sumarrize the plat of this sattire, please?

3. Although I was a newbey on the website, I felt a strange sense of dégà vue when I read the blogg post.

4. At my first enterview for the accounting departmment, my emploier explained their attendance polacy and healthcare benifits.

5. After you loggin, I will uplode the spreidsheet to the netwerk.

6. We're trying to introduce more greene produkts that will help us become a more sustanaible corperation.

7. Viril comtent is important for a website, but it is also good to have a user-freindley serch enjine.

8. The anadote told by the actor at the debuy of his one-man show was so hilarious that we leapt to our feet and shouted "Bravvoa!"

9. If you own a credet card, show fiscall responsibility and pay off your det at the end of each month.

Misspelled Words:

_____ _____ _____ _____

_____ _____ _____ _____

_____ _____ _____ _____

_____ _____ _____ _____

_____ _____ _____

_____ _____ _____ _____

_____ _____ _____ _____

_____ _____ _____ _____

_____ _____ _____ _____

A	F	I	C	I	O	N	A	D	O	P	L	B	X	S	N
N	M	S	U	S	T	A	I	N	A	B	L	E	H	U	O
E	I	I	A	C	O	N	T	E	N	T	N	M	M	M	A
C	N	S	G	T	T	L	A	C	S	I	F	P	P	M	N
D	T	P	E	O	I	A	X	M	G	U	P	L	O	A	D
O	E	R	I	B	D	R	D	N	K	R	O	O	E	R	Z
T	R	E	B	J	E	D	E	B	U	T	E	Y	Y	I	X
E	V	A	W	F	R	H	P	V	R	Q	J	E	F	Z	A
G	I	D	E	R	C	I	A	S	S	A	C	R	N	E	M
C	E	S	N	R	T	J	R	R	T	C	V	I	O	K	I
Z	W	H	A	H	E	E	T	Y	C	I	L	O	P	R	L
Q	A	E	L	D	S	B	M	W	U	V	F	U	D	O	C
U	S	E	R	F	R	I	E	N	D	L	Y	E	G	W	G
K	Y	T	B	E	D	D	N	S	O	D	G	I	N	T	O
V	I	R	A	L	T	G	T	P	R	W	N	V	E	E	L
U	F	N	O	I	T	A	R	O	P	R	O	C	H	N	B

CHAPTER 10 WORD LIST

aficionado (ə-fish-ē-ə-näˊdō)
amigo (ə-mēˊgō)
anecdote (ănˊĭk-dōt)

application (ăp-lĭ-kāʹshŭn)

archetype (ärʹkĭ-tīp)

balance (bălʹəns)

bandwidth (băndʹwĭ*th*)

bankrupt (bănkʹrŭpt)

benefits (bĕnʹə-fĭtz)

blasé (blä-zāʹ)

blog (blôg)

blogosphere (blôgʹō-sfîr)

bourgeois (bôr-zwäʹ)

branding (brăndʹĭng)

bravo (brä-vōʹ)

browser (browʹzər)

cliché (klē-shāʹ)

climax (klīʹmăks)

compatible (kŭm-pătʹĭbəl)

connoisseur (kŏn-nō-sürʹ)

content (kŏnʹtĕnt)

corporation (kôr-pôr-āʹshŭn)

coup de grâce (kü də gräsʹ)

credit (krĕdʹĭt)

cursor (kərʹsər)

database (dāʹtə-bās)

debt (dĕt)

debut (dā-byûʹ)

déjà vu (dā-zhä vüʹ)

department (dē-pärtʹmĕnt)

digital (dĭ-jĭ-təl)

diversity (dī-vərʹsĭ-tē)

download (downʹlōd)

employer (ĕm-ploiʹər)

entrepreneur (ŏn-trə-prə-nüʹər)

exposition (ĕks-pō-zĭsh-ən)

facade (fə-sädʹ)

figurative (fĭgʹûr-ə-tĭv)

fiscal (fĭsʹkəl)

gig (gĭg)

gigabyte (gĭg´ə-bīt)

globalization (glō-bəl-ĭ-zā´shən)

grassroots (grăs-rüts´)

green (grēn)

hard drive (hârd´ drīv)

hyperbole (hī-pər´bŭ-lē)

implement (ĭm´plĭ-mĕnt)

incognito (ĭn-kŏg-nē´tō)

incur (ĭn´kər)

input (ĭn´pŏŏt)

insurance (ĭn-shyûr´ĕns)

interpret (ĭn-tər´prĭt)

interview (ĭn´tər-vyû)

irony (ī´rŭn-ē)

jargon (jär´gən)

keyword (kē´wərd)

laissez-faire (lĕs-zā fâr´)

literal (lĭt´ər-əl)

login (log´ĭn)

malaise (məl-āz´)

mouse (mows)

naïve (nī-ēv´)

network (nĕt´wərk)

newbie (nü´bē)

non sequitur (nŏn sĕ´kwĭt-ər)

online (ŏn´līn)

outsource (owt´sôrs)

passé (pă-sā´)

personification (pər-sŏn´ĭ-fĭ-kā-shən)

plot (plŏt)

policy (pŏl-ə´sē)

procedure (prō-cē´jyûr)

product (prŏ´dŭkt)

protagonist (prō-tăg´ə-nĭst)

pun (pŭn)

references (rĕf′rən-sĭz)

rendezvous (rŏn′dä-vü)

résumé (rĕ′zə–mā)

rhetoric (rĕ′tōr-ĭk)

salary (săl′ə-rē)

satire (să′tī-ər)

search engine (sərch′ ĭn-jĭn)

setting (sĕt′ĭng)

social networking (sō′shəl nĕt′wərk-ĭng)

spiel (shpēl)

spreadsheet (sprĕd′shēt)

stanza (stănz′ə)

sticky (stĭk′ē)

summarize (sŭm′ər-īz)

sustainable (sŭs-tān′ə-bəl)

text (tĕkst′ĭng)

theme (thēm)

tipping point (tĭp′ĭng point)

tone (tōn)

transparent (trăns-pâr′ĕnt)

upload (ŭp′lōd)

user-friendly (yû′zər frĕnd′lē)

username (yû′zər-nām)

vegan (vē′gən)

vendetta (vĕn-dĕt′ə)

viral (vī′rəl)

virtual (vər′chü′əl)

ANSWERS

1. **d. credit.** *Insurance* is more like a fund that an employee can draw from than money due to a person. A *network* is a technology term, and a *product* is something produced by a company. The answer is choice **d.**
2. **a. climax.** *Anecdote* is a humorous story, while choice *archetype* is an original model of a character. A *vegan* is a term for a person or food product, so the correct answer here is choice **a.**

3. **b. grassroots.** Although *globalization* involves people across the world, and something *viral* is spread by people around the world, neither of these is really defined as "involving the common people." *Online* refers to anyone or anything on a computer or the Internet, so the answer is choice **b**.

4. **b. incognito.** An *anecdote* is a story, so choice **a** cannot be correct. Someone who is *naïve* is childishly innocent, and *implement* is a verb; therefore, the answer is choice **b**.

5. **b. user-friendly.** The term *keyword* does not refer to software or hardware. A *résumé* is a piece of paper listening one's job qualifications, and *compatible* means "works together well." The answer is choice **b**.

6. **a. jargon.** A *policy* is a company's rule, not its vocabulary. *Keywords* might seem correct, but they are words used in search engines, not vocabulary words used by businesses. A *corporation* is another word for a company, so the answer is choice **a**.

7. **d. input.** An *interview* is a discussion held by someone attempting to get a job. *Downloading* means copying files from a network location to a computer, and *rhetoric* is a literary term related to speech. The correct answer is choice **d**.

8. **c. plot.** Although these are all literary terms, the only word that describes the course of events in the story is choice **c**.

9. **a. browser.** These are all computer terms, but a *network* is a linked group of computers, a *search engine* is a program used to search for files, and *upload* is a verb. Therefore, the answer is choice **a**.

10. **d. cliché.** *Spiel* is related to speech, but it does not mean "overused phrase." *Satire* and *pun* are both forms of humor, so the answer here is choice **d**.

11. **passé.** *Passé* is pronounced like *passay*, but it is a foreign word in which the *ay* sound is spelled *é*.

12. **bankrupt.** Someone who is *bankrupt* would have nothing in the *bank*.

13. **debt.** The word *debt* has a silent *b*.

14. **anecdote.** An *anecdote* is an entertaining story.

15. **spreadsheet.** *Spreadsheet* is a compound word.

16. **stanza.** *Stanza* is pronounced just like it is spelled.

17. **content.** *Content*, a noun meaning "substantive information," is pronounced with the accent on the first syllable. The adjective *content*, with the accent on the second syllable, means "happy."

18. **username.** *Username* is all one word.

19. **browser.** Remember that you would *browse* the Internet with a *browser*.

20. **naïve.** The double dots above the *i* in *naïve* indicate that the *i* has two sounds; long *i* (ī) and long *e* (ē). The word is pronounced (nī-ēv).

21. **compatible.** There are no double letters in *compatible*.

22. **sustainable.** If something is *able* to be *sustained*, it is *sustainable*.

23. **fiscal.** Try to remember that *fiscal* means almost the same as *financial*.

24. **hyperbole.** The *-bole* in *hyperbole* is actually pronounced like *bully*.

25. **entrepreneur.** This is a difficult word to remember because it is French and does not carry any recognizable English suffixes or prefixes. Notice that the word *connoisseur* has the same ending; *-eur* is the French equivalent of *-er*.

Game Time: Search-A-Word Solution

Misspelled Words:

amigo	employer	viral
aficionado	policy	content
climax	benefits	user-friendly
summarize	login	search engine
plot	upload	anecdote
satire	spreadsheet	debut
newbie	network	bravo
déjà vu	green	credit
blog	products	fiscal
interview	sustainable	debt
department	corporation	

A	F	I	C	I	O	N	A	D	O	P	L	B	X	S	N
N	M	S	U	S	T	A	I	N	A	B	L	E	H	U	O
E	I	I	A	C	O	N	T	E	N	T	N	M	M	M	A
C	N	S	G	T	T	L	A	C	S	I	F	P	P	M	N
D	T	P	E	O	I	A	X	M	G	U	P	L	O	A	D
O	E	R	I	B	D	R	D	N	K	R	O	O	E	R	Z
T	R	E	B	J	E	D	E	B	U	T	E	Y	Y	I	X
E	V	A	W	F	R	H	P	V	R	Q	J	E	F	Z	A
G	I	D	E	R	C	I	A	S	S	A	C	R	N	E	M
C	E	S	N	R	T	J	R	R	T	C	V	I	O	K	I
Z	W	H	A	H	E	E	T	Y	C	I	L	O	P	R	L
Q	A	E	L	D	S	B	M	W	U	V	F	U	D	O	C
U	S	E	R	F	R	I	E	N	D	L	Y	E	G	W	G
K	Y	T	B	E	D	D	N	S	O	D	G	I	N	T	O
V	I	R	A	L	T	G	T	P	R	W	N	V	E	E	L
U	F	N	O	I	T	A	R	O	P	R	O	C	H	N	B

Posttest

The following posttest measures your knowledge of the spelling fundamentals covered in this book. Try to complete the test without referring to the book. Then, check your answers. If you find yourself having difficulty with any particular skill, revisit that chapter.

SENTENCE COMPLETION

This exercise tests your ability to recognize the correct spelling of a word. Each sentence is followed by four answer choices. Choose the answer choice that is spelled correctly and makes the most sense in the sentence.

1. Corinne is the most _____ person I know.
    a. fashionble
    b. fashioneble
    c. fashionible
    d. fashionable

2. He has a lovely Italian _____.
    a. axcent
    b. accent
    c. aksent
    d. acsent

3. The horse drank from a _____.
   a. trough
   b. troufh
   c. trouf
   d. troufgh

4. *Stick* and *wick* are two words that _____.
   a. ryme
   b. rhime
   c. rhyme
   d. rime

5. The kids all go to the _____ for recess.
   a. play-ground
   b. playground
   c. play ground
   d. playeground

6. The first year of the new _____ was actually 2001, not 2000.
   a. milennium
   b. millennium
   c. milenium
   d. millenium

7. Is your new camera _____ with this operating system?
   a. compatable
   b. compateible
   c. compattible
   d. compatible

8. This _____ has to be the strangest situation I've ever seen.
   a. surely
   b. shurely
   c. surly
   d. shirly

9. I've recently become an _____ of old movies.
   a. afishinado
   b. afficianado
   c. aficionado
   d. afitionaddo

10. My friend Jesse has a lot of _____ riding horses.
    a. expereince
    b. experiance
    c. expereence
    d. experience

CHOOSE THE RIGHT SPELLING

Circle the italicized word that is spelled correctly in each of the following sentences.

11. The baby (*smeered/smeared*) chocolate on the tablecloth.

12. Frankie gets along well with his (*mother in law/mother-in-law*).

13. Janine took the story seriously, but I thought it was meant as (*satire/satyre*).

14. (*Spagetti/spaghetti*) is one of my favorite foods.

15. When the company (*impliments/implements*) the new vacation policies, we will all get more time off.

16. Maria got into an (*argument/arguement*) with her sister last night.

17. This jacket is (*reversible/reversable*).

18. My older brother spends a lot of time staring at his (*rephlection/reflection*) in the mirror.

19. The race-car driver executed an incredible (*maneuver/manuever*).

20. The lake is filled with perch and (*trowt/trout*).

HOMONYMS AND COMMONLY CONFUSED WORDS

The following sentences contain words that are commonly confused. Circle the spelling of the italicized word that best completes the sentence.

21. My kite was stuck on the (*bough/bow*) of the tree.

22. Julie's house is (*further/farther*) down the road than my house.

23. The king's (*rain/reign/rein*) was a difficult period in the country's history.

24. At the roadside stand, the vendor (*peddles/pedals*) his wares.

25. We must go (*foreword/forward*) to reach our destination.

26. It took my dog, King, a few days to (*adopt/adapt*) to his new home.

27. The word *apple* (*precedes/proceeds*) the word *attitude* in the dictionary.

28. We still had an (*access/excess*) amount of cookies left over after dessert.

29. It can help to (*very/vary*) your activity if you're getting bored.

30. The couple took a walk on the (*pier/peer*) after dinner.

SUFFIXES

Combine the following base words with the endings indicated. Write the new word in the blank space.

31. silly + -ness = _____

32. compel + -ing = _____

33. romantic + -ly = _____

34. place + -ment = _____

35. thought + -ful = _____

36. lazy + -est = _____

37. enjoy + -ment = _____

38. flip + -ant = _____

39. reduce + -ible = _____

40. connect + -ive = _____

PLURALS

Correctly spell the plural forms of the following words.

Singular	Plural
41. crash	_____
42. half	_____
43. banjo	_____
44. cattle	_____
45. person	_____

Singular	Plural
46. bunny	_____
47. matrix	_____
48. stray	_____
49. style	_____
50. tomato	_____

VERB CONJUGATIONS

Write the present participle, past tense, and past participle of each of the following words.

Present Tense	Present Participle	Past Tense	Past Participle
51. trap	_____	_____	_____
52. enjoy	_____	_____	_____
53. cost	_____	_____	_____
54. sell	_____	_____	_____
55. steal	_____	_____	_____
56. lose	_____	_____	_____
57. rile	_____	_____	_____
58. lead	_____	_____	_____

Present Tense	Present Participle	Past Tense	Past Participle
59. become	_____	_____	_____
60. ring	_____	_____	_____

ANSWERS

Sentence Completion

1. **d. fashionable.** (Chapter 3) The *-able* ending is usually added to words that can stand on their own, like *fashion* (*fashionable*) or *person* (*personable*).

2. **b. accent.** (Chapter 5) *Accent* is the rare word with an *acc* combination in which the letter *c* makes both a soft sound and a hard sound.

3. **a. trough.** (Chapter 5) The consonant digraph *gh* sometimes makes an *f* sound.

4. **c. rhyme.** (Chapter 4; Chapter 5) The letter *y* can sometimes make a long *i* sound, as it does in the word *rhyme*. Remember that *rhyme* also has a silent *h*.

5. **b. playground.** (Chapter 3) *Playground* is a compound word that does not require a hyphen.

6. **b. millennium.** (Chapter 9) *Millennium* is one of the 201 most often misspelled words. The prefix *mill-/milli-* can be found in many other words, such as *million, millisecond,* and *millipede*. The root *enn* is in the same family as the root *ann*, which can be found in the words *annual* and *anniversary*.

7. **d. compatible.** (Chapter 10; Chapter 3) The word *compatible* is a buzz-word meaning "able to work together." It comes from a root that cannot stand on its own as a word, so it has an *-ible* ending.

8. **a. surely.** (Chapter 4) *Surely* is an r-controlled word. The letter *r* has a unique effect on the pronunciation of vowels.

9. **c. aficionado.** (Chapter 10) *Aficionado* is an Italian word that is commonly used in English. It can be difficult to remember how to spell foreign words, because English rules do not always apply. These words generally just have to be memorized.

10. **d. experience.** (Chapter 9) *Experience* is one of the 201 most often misspelled words in the English language.

Choose the Right Spelling

11. **smeared.** (Chapter 4) *Smear* is an r-controlled word. The letter combination *ear* often has an ē + r sound.

12. **mother-in-law.** (Chapter 3) *Mother-in-law* is a hyphenated compound word.

13. **satire.** (Chapter 10) *Satire* is a literary term that describes a style of comedic writing.

14. **spaghetti.** (Chapter 5) The *gh* combination can make a number of different sounds. When it is followed immediately by a vowel, it is generally pronounced as a hard *g*.

15. **implements.** (Chapter 10) *Implement* is a business word. Remember that the schwa sound in *implement* is spelled with an *e*.

16. **argument.** (Chapter 9) *Argument* is one of the words that looks like it should have a silent *e* but does not.

17. **reversible.** (Chapter 3; Chapter 6) Usually, *-ible* is added to words that do not stand on their own, like *visible* or *feasible*. *Reversible* is a common exception. Drop the silent *e* when adding the *-ible* ending.

18. **reflection.** (Chapter 5) *Fl* is a common two letter blend that is found in words like *reflection*, *flower*, and *fluid*.

19. **maneuver.** (Chapter 9) The word *maneuver* is unusual because the silent *e* comes before the *u*. It is one of the 201 most commonly misspelled words in the English language.

20. **trout.** (Chapter 4) The letter combination *o* + *u* is a diphthong that produces an *ow* sound.

Homonyms and Commonly Confused Words
(Chapter 2)

21. **bough.** The words *bow* and *bough* are homonyms. The word *bow* means "to bend at the waist in a show of respect," while the word *bough* means "a tree branch."

22. **farther.** *Farther* and *further* are frequently confused. The word *farther* refers to distance, so in this case, *farther* is the correct choice.

23. **reign.** *Reign, rain,* and *rein* are homonyms. The choice that fits the this sentence is *reign,* meaning "rule."

24. **peddles.** To *pedal* is to work a foot pedal, as on a bike. To *peddle* means "to sell."

25. **forward.** A *foreword* is the introduction to a book. *Forward* means "to move ahead."

26. **adapt.** To *adopt* means "to take as one's own," while to *adapt* is "to change." It would take a dog a few days to *adapt* to its new home.

27. **precedes.** *Proceeds* are profits, while *precede* is a verb meaning "come before." This sentence calls for a verb meaning "comes before," so *precedes* is the correct answer.

28. **excess.** Many people confuse the words *access* and *excess.* Just remember that *excess* means "extra," and you should be able to figure out the correct answer for this sentence.

29. **vary.** *Very* is an adverb meaning "really," while *vary* is a verb meaning "change."

30. **pier.** *Pier* and *peer* are frequently confused homonyms. A *peer* is an equal, however; the only choice that makes sense in this case is *pier.*

Suffixes

(Chapter 6)

31. **silliness.** When combining words that end in consonant + *-y* combinations with suffixes, change the *-y* to an *i* before adding the suffix.

32. **compelling.** Multiple-syllable words that end in consonant + vowel + consonant combinations double the final consonant when adding suffixes that begin with vowels if the accent is on the final syllable.

33. **romantically.** When adding the suffix *-ly* to a base word that ends in *-ic,* the suffix is changed to *-ally.*

34. **placement.** If a word ends in a silent *e* and the suffix begins with a consonant, no change is required.

35. **thoughtful.** No change is required when adding a suffix that begins with a consonant to a word that ends with a consonant.

36. **laziest.** When combining words that end in consonant + *-y* combinations with suffixes, change the *-y* to an *i* before adding the suffix.

37. **enjoyment.** Words that end in vowel + *-y* combinations do not change the *-y* to an *i* when adding suffixes.

38. **flippant**. Words that end in consonant + vowel + consonant combinations double the final consonant when adding suffixes that begin with vowels.

39. **reducible**. When a word ends in a silent *e* and the suffix begins with a vowel, drop the final *e* when adding the suffix.

40. **connective**. If a base word ends in multiple consonants, no change is required when adding the suffix.

Plurals
(Chapter 7)

41. **crashes**. Add *-es* to nouns that end in *-sh*.

42. **halves**. Most words that end in *-f* or *-fe* change the *-f* or *-fe* to a *v* before adding *-es*.

43. **banjos**. Most words that add in *-o* add *-es* when forming the plural, but *banjo* is an exception.

44. **cattle**. Some animal names are the same in the singular and plural.

45. **people**. *Person/people* is an irregular noun that just has to be memorized.

46. **bunnies**. When a noun ends in consonant + *-y*, change the *-y* to an *i* before forming the plural.

47. **matrices**. *Matrix* is a technical word ending in *-ix*; the plural is formed by changing the *-ix* to an *ic* and adding *-es*.

48. **strays**. Add *-s* to form the plural of words that end in vowel + *-y*.

49. **styles**. Add *-s* to words that end in silent *e*.

50. **tomatoes**. Words that end in *-o* generally add *-es* when forming the plural.

Verb Conjugations
(Chapter 8)

51. **trapping/trapped/trapped**. *Trap* is a regular verb. Remember to double the final consonant when adding *-ing* and *-ed* endings to words that end in consonant + vowel + consonant endings.

52. **enjoying/enjoyed/enjoyed**. *Enjoy* is a regular verb that adds *-ing* and *-ed* endings with no change to the base word.

53. **costing/cost/cost**. *Cost* is an irregular verb that does not change between the present tense, past tense, and past participle forms.

54. **selling/sold/sold.** *Sell* is an irregular verb that has the same past tense and past participle forms.

55. **stealing/stole/stolen.** *Steal* is an irregular verb with unique past tense and past participle forms.

56. **losing/lost/lost.** *Lost* is an irregular verb that has the same past tense and past participle forms.

57. **riling/riled/riled.** *Rile* is a regular verb. Remember to drop the silent *e* when adding suffixes that begin with vowels to regular verbs.

58. **leading/led/led.** *Lead* is an irregular verb with the same past tense and past participle forms. Be careful to remember that *read* and *lead* conjugate differently; the past tense and past participle of *read* are both *read*, while the past tense and past participles of *lead* are both *led*.

59. **becoming/became/become.** *Become* is an irregular verb with unique past tense and past participle forms.

60. **ringing/rang/rung.** *Ring* is an irregular verb with unique past tense and past participle forms.

Appendix A
Master Word List

This list contains all of the spelling words and terms that have been featured in this book.

A
abandon
absence
abundance
accept
acceptable
access
accessible
accidentally
accommodate
accomplish
account
achieve
achievement
acquaintance
acquire
across
action
adapt
address

adjective

adopt

adverb

affect

affection

affix

aficionado

again

aggravate

all ready

all right

allege

allowed

aloud

already

alveolar

always

amazement

amiable

amigo

among

analysis

anecdote

annoyance

annual

apparent

appearance

application

archetype

argument

ascend

asks

assure

attendance

auction

audible

authority
awareness

B
balance
bandwidth
bankrupt
bare
bargain
base
basically
bear
bearable
beat
beet
beige
believe
beneficial
benefits
beside
besides
between
bilabial
biscuit
blasé
blog
blogosphere
board
boastful
boisterous
bored
bough
bought
boundary
bourgeois
bow

boxes

brake

branding

bravo

breadth

break

breath

breathe

broke

broken

browser

buffaloes

bulletin

business

C

calendar

canceled

candidate

capital

capitol

category

ceaselessly

cell

cemetery

changeable

children

chronic

cite

cliché

climax

climbs

clothes

coarse

coincidence

collectible

colonel

column

comfortable

comforting

commitment

committed

committee

communicate

compatible

complement

compliment

composed

compound

conceive

concerned

concierge

confide

congratulations

conjugate

connoisseur

conscience

conscientious

conscious

consistent

consistently

consonant

consonant blends

content

conveyer

cooperatively

corporation

correspondence

council

counsel

counterpart

coup de grâce

course

courteous

courtesy

credible

credit

critiques

crowd

crwth

crypt

cursor

cwm

D

database

daughter

dear

debt

debut

decay

declined

deer

defendant

definite

déjà vu

department

dependent

descend

desperate

destructive

development

die

digestible

digital

digraph

diphthong

disposing

disable

disastrous

discipline

discrepancy

disinterested

dissatisfied

diversity

download

drawing

draws

driving

dropped

drought

drunk

dual

duel

dumbbell

dye

dynamic

E

earmuffs

easels

easily

eating

ecstasy

edible

effect

eighth

elicit

eligible

embarrass

employer

enjoyable

ensure

enthralled

entrepreneur
envelop
envelope
envious
environment
equipment
exceed
except
excess
excusable
executive
exercise
exhilarate
existence
experience
exposition
extraordinary
extremely

F
facade
fair
familiar
fare
farther
fashionable
fatten
feasible
feat
February
feet
fiery
fifth
figurative
find
fined

first person
fiscal
fished
fix
flanked
flight
follicle
foreign
foreword
forfeit
forward
foundation
freight
from
fulfill
further

G
gait
gate
gateways
gauge
generally
gig
gigabyte
globalization
gnashed
goodness
gracious
grammar
grassroots
grate
grateful
great
green
grief

guarantee
guidance
gulfs

H
happily
harass
hard drive
hassle
hatches
heal
heel
height
heroes
homographs
homonyms
homophones
hoping
horrible
hotter
humorous
hyperbole
hyphenated

I
ignorance
illicit
imaginary
immediate
implement
incite
inclined
incognito
incredible
incredulous
incur

indebted

independence

independent

indices

indispensable

inexcusable

infamous

infinitive

input

insight

instantaneously

instinctual

instructions

insufficient

insurance

insure

intelligence

intemperate

interjection

interpret

interview

introduce

invisible

irony

irregular verbs

irrelevant

irreplaceable

irresistible

J

jargon

jealous

jewelry

judgment

juvenile

K
keyword
knives
knowledgeable

L
labiodental
laissez-faire
laughed
lazier
lead
led
leisure
length
let
library
license
lightning
linguadental
literal
loan
loaves
login
lone
loose
lose
lunches
lynx

M
made
maintenance
malaise
manageable
maneuver
may be

maybe
media
medieval
millennium
miniature
minuscule
miscellaneous
mischievous
misspell
mnemonic
modems
mouse
murmur
muscle
mysterious
myth

N
naïve
narrator
navies
necessary
negotiate
neighbor
network
newbie
ninety
ninth
non sequitur
noticeable
noun

O
obvious
occasion
occasionally

occur

occurrence

omnipotent

omnivore

omnivorous

online

opportunity

opposed

outrageous

outsource

ova

overdo

overdue

P

pain

palatal

pane

pantries

parallel

paralyses

parentheses

participle

passé

passed

past

past participle

past tense

pastime

peace

peal

pedal

peddle

peel

peer

performance

permanent

perseverance

persistence

personal

personification

personnel

pharmacy

phonics

piece

pier

pitiful

plain

plane

planning

platter

played

pleasant

plot

plural

policy

politicians

possess

possession

practically

precede

predetermined

preferred

prefix

preparation

prepare

preposterous

present participle

present tense

presumed

prevented

preyed

pride
principal
principle
privilege
probably
procedure
proceed
proceeds
product
pronunciation
protagonist
proved
pun

Q
quantity
questionnaire

R
rain
rashes
really
recede
receipt
receive
recess
recognize
recommend
reference
references
referral
referred
regular verbs
reign
rein
relaxant

relevant
rendezvous
repetition
replacing
repulsive
resell
resemblance
respect
respectable
restaurant
résumé
resumed
reversible
revert
rhetoric
rhyme
rhythm
riches
ridiculous
right
riled
rite
roommate
roost
root
runner

S

safety
salary
satellites
satire
saying
scary
schedule
schwa

search engine
second person
secondary
sell
separate
sergeant
setting
shareholder
shielded
shy
sigh
similar
singular
site
sleigh
smiling
soar
social networking
sore
spiel
splashing
spreading
spreadsheet
stanza
started
stationary
stationery
stepbrothers
sticky
stimuli
studios
study
subtle
succeed
success
succumb

suffix
summarize
supersede
supplies
susceptible
sustainable
suture
sweaters
syllables

T
tail
taken
tale
task
tasty
team
teem
temperature
text
than
theme
then
thief
thieves
third person
throughout
tipping point
tomatoes
tone
trafficking
tranquil
transform
transmit
transparent
tremendous

tried
trigraph
tripped
twelfth
tyranny

U
umbrellas
unable
undisputed
undoubtedly
unemployed
unemployment
uninterested
unlikely
unremittingly
until
upload
usable
user-friendly
username
usually

V
vacuum
vain
valuable
vary
vegan
vein
velar
vendetta
vengeance
ventriloquist
verb
vertebrae

very
viral
virtual
visible
vision
vowels

W
waist
waits
wanted
warranty
was
waste
weigh
weird
wherever
whine
who
who's
whom
whose
why
wicker
wright
write

Appendix B
Glossary of English Terms and Difficult Words

adjective (ăd´jəkt-ĭv) *n.* the part of speech that modifies a noun or pronoun

adverb (ăd´vərb) *n.* the part of speech that modifies a verb, an adjective, another adverb, a clause, or a sentence

affix (ă´fĭkz) *n.* a group of letters that change or enhance a root's meaning

aficionado (ə-fĭsh-ē-ə-nä´dō) *n.* a person who likes, knows about, and is devoted to a particular activity or thing

alveolar (ăl-vē-ō´lər) *adj.* consonant shape made when the tip of the tongue near the back of the upper teeth

amigo (ə-mē´gō) *n.* friend

anecdote (ăn´ĭk-dōt) *n.* a short account of an interesting or humorous incident

application (ăp-lĭ-kā´shŭn) *n.* a software program that lets you complete a task on your computer, such as word processing, listening to music, or viewing a web page

archetype (är´kĭ-tīp) *n.* an original model or type after which other similar things are patterned

balance (băl´əns) *n.* the difference between money available and money owed

bandwidth (bănd´wĭth) *n.* the capacity for sending information through an Internet connection

bankrupt (băngk´rŭpt) *n.* the legal state of being unable to pay ones debts

base (bās) *n.* the most basic form of a word from which all affixes have been removed

benefits (běn´ə-fĭtz) *n.* anything offered by an employer in addition to salary, including health insurance, vacation days, and sick days

bilabial (bī-lāb´ē-əl) *adj.* consonant shape made when the lips press together and pull apart

blasé (blä-zā´) *adj.* boring as a result of overexposure

blog (blôg) *n.* or *v.* short for "weblog," an online diary or collection of frequently updated information; or the process of updating that information

blogosphere (blôg´ō-sfîr) *n.* a collective term for the community of weblogs and bloggers

boisterous (boist´ər-əs) *adj.* loud

bourgeois (bôr-zwä´) *adj.* showing excessive concern for materialistic goods

branding (brănd´ĭng) *n.* a marketing term, the definition of a company for advertising purposes

bravo (brä-vō´) *int.* great job

browser (brow´zər) *n.* the program a user uses to look at files on the Web

cliché (klē-shā´) *n.* a phrase or saying that has been overused and, as a result, has little significance

climax (klī´măks) *n.* the crucial moment in a story

compatible (kŭm-păt´ĭbəl) *adj.* able to work together, often used to describe software or computer devices

compound words (kŏm-pownd wərdz) *n. pl.* words composed of more than one independent words

concierge (kŏn-sē-ârzh´) *n.* a worker in a hotel who is responsible for assisting hotel guests

conjugate (kŏn´jə-gāt) *v.* to recite or display all forms of a verb

connoisseur (kŏn-nō-sür´) *n.* one who knows a lot about a certain subject

consonant (kŏn´sən-ənt) *n.* one of the 21 letters in the English alphabet that is not a vowel

consonant blends (kŏn´sən-ənt blĕndz) *n. pl.* consonant combinations in which the letters keep their original sounds

content (kŏn´tĕnt) *n.* substantive information

corporation (kôr-pôr-ā´shŭn) *n.* a company that is legally treated as an individual

coup de grâce (kü də grâs´) *n.* the final triumph

credit (krĕd´ĭt) *n.* money due to a person or business

cursor (kər´sər) *n.* a symbol, usually a blinking line or arrow, that shows the location of an input device on the screen

database (dā´tə-bās) *n.* an organizational system using tables that helps a computer quickly retrieve pieces of information

debt (dĕt) *n.* money owed by a person or business

debut (dā-byû´) *n.* a first appearance

déjà vu (dā-zhä vü´) *n.* the feeling that one has been in a situation before

department (dē-pärt´mĕnt) *n.* a smaller division within a company

digital (dĭ-jĭ-təl) *adj.* the description of any electronic device that uses numbers to calculate information

digraphs (dī´grăfs) *n. pl.* two-letter combinations that make a single sound

diphthong (dĭf´thông or dĭp´thông) *n.* a complex vowel sound that is created when two vowel sounds are blended together

diversity (dī-vər´sĭ-tē) *n.* a state consisting of a variety of different elements; often used in referring to race or ethnicity

download (down´lōd) *v.* the process of copying files from an outside source to your computer or network location

employer (ĕm-ploi´ər) *n.* business or individual for whom an employee works

entrepreneur (ŏn-trə-prə-nü´ər) *n.* a person who starts his or her own business

exposition (ĕks-pō-zĭsh-ən) *n.* the part of the story that sets up the plot

facade (fə-säd´) *n.* a false front

figurative (fĭg´ûr-ə-tĭv) *adj.* not literal

first person (fərst pər´sən) *n.* the point of view expressed by the words *I* (singular) or *we* (plural)

fiscal (fĭs´kəl) *adj.* financial

gigabyte (gĭg´ə-bīt) or **gig** (gĭg) *n.* a measure of storage capacity equal to one billion bytes; currently the predominant measure of hard drive space

globalization (glō-bəl-ĭ-zā´shən) *n.* the state of extending to all parts of the globe, often used in reference to economic matters

grassroots (grăs-rüts´) *adj.* involving the common people

green (grēn) *adj.* environmentally friendly

hard drive (hârd´ drīv) *n.* the part of a computer on which information is stored

hard sound (hârd sownd) *n.* the sound produced by the letter *c* in *crust* or the letter *g* in *game*

homographs (hŏ´mə-grăfs) *n. pl.* words that have an identical spelling to other words but have different meanings and different pronunciations

homonyms (hŏ´mə-nĭmz) *n. pl.* words that have the same pronunciation but different meanings

homophones (hŏ´mə-fōnz) *n. pl.* words that are spelled differently but have the same pronunciation and different meanings

hyperbole (hī-pər´bŭ-lē) *n.* intentional exaggeration

hyphenated words (hī´fən-āt-ĭd wərdz) *n. pl.* words or phrases that are connected with a hyphen

implement (ĭm´plĭ-mĕnt) *v.* to put into effect

incognito (ĭn-kŏg-nē´tō) *adj.* or *adv.* with one's identity concealed

incredulous (ĭn-krĕd´yû-ləs) *adj.* amazed; awestruck; disbelieving

incur (ĭn´kər) *v.* to come into or acquire, usually undesirably

infinitive (ĭn-fĭn´ə-tĭv) *n.* the form of a verb using the word *to*, as in *to jump* or *to sing*

input (ĭn´pŏŏt) *v.* the process of entering information into a computer

insurance (ĭn-shyûr´ĕns) *n.* a coverage plan in which an individual pays a regular fee in exchange for future services

intemperate (ĭn-tĕmp´ər-ĭt) *adj.* unrestrained

interjection (ĭn-tər-jĕk´shŭn) *n.* a word used to express emotion

interpret (ĭn-tər´prĭt) *v.* to explain the meaning of

interview (ĭn´tər-vyû) *n.* a formal meeting set up between an employer and employee when attempting to be hired for a job

irony (ī´rŭn-ē) *n.* the use of words to express something different from the literal meaning

irregular verb (îr´rĕg-yû-lər vŭrb) *n.* a verb that does not follow the most common conjugation rules

jargon (jär′gən) *n.* the specialized vocabulary of an industry or group

keyword (kē′wərd) *n.* a word connected to a larger concept used to simplify web searches

labiodental (lāb′ē-ō-dĕnt-əl) *adj.* consonant shape made when the lower lip presses against the upper teeth

laissez-faire (lĕs-zā fâr′) *n.* a policy opposing government control of economic matters except in the case of maintaining peace and the concept of property

linguadental (lĭng′gwə-dĕnt-əl) *adj.* consonant shape made when the middle of the tongue presses near the back of the upper teeth

literal (lĭt′ər-əl) *adj.* the actual meaning

login (log′ĭn) *n.* the process of identifying oneself to a computer or network location, usually by entering a username and password

long vowels (lông vow′əlz) *n. pl.* vowels that have the same pronunciation as their names, as in the *a* in *bake* or the *i* in *bike*

malaise (məl-āz′) *n.* a feeling of mental unease or discomfort

mnemonic (nĭ-mŏn′ĭk) *n.* a phrase or rhyme that is used to make memorization easier

mouse (mows) *n.* a sliding input device with one or two buttons used to operate a cursor on a computer screen

naïve (nī-ēv′) *adj.* innocent, simple, lacking knowledge of the world

network (nĕt′wərk) *n.* a group of two or more computers linked together

newbie (nü′bē) *n.* someone who is doing something for the first time

non sequitur (nŏn sĕ′kwĭt-ər) *n.* a statement that has no connection to the previous statement or idea

noun (nown) *n.* the part of speech that names a person, place, thing, or idea

omnipotent (ŏm-nĭ′pō′tĭnt) *adj.* all-powerful

omnivore (äm-ni-vor) *n.* an animal that eats either plants or animals

online (ŏn´līn) *adj.* connected to a computer or network

outsource (owt´sôrs) *v.* to contract jobs to outside workers

palatal (pāl´ə-təl) *adj.* consonant shape made when the front of the tongue touches the hard palate

participle (pär´tə-sĭp´əl) *n.* a form of a verb used as an adjective

passé (pă-sā´) *adj.* out of fashion

past participle (păst pär´tə-sĭp´əl) *n.* a form of a verb used as an adjective in the past tense

past tense (păst tĕns) *adj.* the expression of action that happened in the past

personification (pər-sŏn´ĭ-fĭ-kā-shən) *n.* the act of giving an inanimate object or animal humanlike properties

plot (plŏt) *n.* the course of events in a story

plural (plərəl) *adj.* multiple

policy (pŏl-ə´sē) *n.* a course of action; a rule

prefix (prē´fĭkz) *n.* a group of letters found at the beginning of a root that change or enhance the root's meaning

present participle (prĕz´ənt pär´tə-sĭp´əl) *n.* a form of a verb used as an adjective in the present tense with an -*ing* ending

present tense (prĕz´ənt tĕns) *adj.* the expression of action that is happening now or continuously

procedure (prō-cē´jyûr) *n.* a way of doing something

product (prŏ´dŭkt) *n.* a thing being produced or manufactured

protagonist (prō-tăg´ə-nĭst) *n.* the main character in a story

pun (pŭn) *n.* play on words

r-controlled vowels (är-kŭn-trōld´ vow´əlz) *n. pl.* vowels that are coupled with the letter *r*

references (rĕf´rən-sĭz) *n.* a group of people presented by a potential employee to an employer who can report on the potential employee's strengths and weaknesses

regular verb (rĕg´yû-lər vŭrb) *n.* a verb that follows the most common conjugation rules

rendezvous (rŏn´dā-vü) *n.* meeting or *v.* to meet

résumé (rĕ´zə–mā) *n.* a printed overview of one's previous job experience

rhetoric (rĕ´tōr-ĭk) *n.* style of speaking

root (rüt) *n.* the syllable or syllables that contain the fundamental meaning of a word

salary (săl´ə-rē) *n.* the amount a job pays, usually figured as an annual amount

satire (să´tī-ər) *n.* a literary style in which important topics are made to look ridiculous through the use of humor

schwa (shwä) *n.* the sound a vowel makes when it is unstressed in an unstressed syllable

search engine (sərch´ ĭn-jĭn) *n.* a program that searches documents, websites, and databases by keywords and returns a list of related information

second person (sĕk´ənd pər´sən) *n.* the point of view expressed by the word *you*

sensory verbs (sĕnz´ər-ē vərbz) *n. pl.* verbs that are related to the senses— touch, taste, smell, sound, and sight

setting (sĕt´ĭng) *n.* the environment or location in which a story takes place

short vowels (shôrt vow´əlz) *n. pl.* vowels that are pronounced with a clipped sound in the back of the throat, as in the *a* in *apple* or the *i* in *big*

singular (sĭng´gyû-lər) *adj.* one

social networking (sō′shəl nĕt′wərk-ĭng) *v.* the use of a website to connect with people who share common interests or qualities

soft sound (sôft sownd) *n.* the sound produced by the letter *c* in the word *cent* or the letter *g* in the word *gel*

spiel (shpēl) *n.* talk given for the purpose of luring an audience or selling a product

spreadsheet (sprĕd′shēt) *n.* a bookkeeping program that displays data in rows and columns, or any individual document created by that program

stanza (stănz′ə) *n.* a group of lines in a poem

sticky (stĭk′ē) *adj.* attracting viewers or readers

suffix (sŭ′fĭkz) *n.* a group of letters found at the end of a root that change or enhance the root's meaning or change the word's part of speech

summarize (sŭm′ər-īz) *v.* to highlight the most important details

sustainable (sŭs-tān′ə-bəl) *adj.* capable of being continued with minimal long-term environmental effects

suture (sü′chər) *n.* a medical stitch

syllable (sĭl′ə-bəl) *n.* a single letter or group of letters that represent an uninterrupted sound

text (tĕkst′ĭng) *v.* to send a message by text message, usually on a cell phone

theme (thēm) *n.* the main idea of a story

third person (thərd pər′sən) *n.* the point of view expressed by the words *he* or *she* (singular) or *they* (plural)

tipping point (tĭp′ĭng point) *n.* the moment from which there is no return

tone (tōn) *n.* the feeling of a story

transparent (trăns-pâr′ĕnt) *adj.* open about operating procedures

trigraphs (trī´grăfs) *n. pl.* three-letter combinations that make a single sound

unremittingly (ŭn-rē-mĭt´ĭng-lē) *adv.* relentlessly

upload (ŭp´lōd) *v.* the process of copying to from an outside source from your computer or network location

user-friendly (yû´zər frĕnd´lē) *adj.* computer software or hardware that easily used by someone with limited knowledge

username (yû´zər-nām) *n.* a nickname used to log on to a computer, website, or network location

vegan (vē´gən) *n.* or *adj.* someone who does not eat any animal-derived foods or use any animal byproducts; description of a food item or product containing no anima-derived ingredients or byproducts

velar (vē´lər) *adj.* consonant shape made when the back of the tongue touches the upper palate

vendetta (vĕn-dĕt´ə) *n.* a grudge or feud characterized by acts of retaliation

ventriloquist (vĕn-trĭl´ō-kwĭst) *n.* an entertainer who projects his or her voice so that the sound appears to come from elsewhere, usually a dummy or puppet

verb (vŭrb) *n.* the part of speech that names an action

viral (vī´rəl) *adj.* an online phenomenon that duplicates like a virus, getting passed around between through e-mail or word-of-mouth

virtual (vər´chü´əl) *adj.* carried on through a computer

vowel (vow´əl) *n.* as a sound that is produced without blocking the passage of air from the throat; the letters *a, e, i, o, u,* and sometimes *y*

Appendix C
Pronunciation Guide

ă   *a* as in **a**pple

ā   *a* as in **a**ce

ä   *a* as in st**a**r

âr   *ar* as in c**are**

ə   *a* as in **a**bout, *e* as in th**e**, *i* as in penc**i**l, *o* as in bish**o**p, *u* as in s**u**pply

b   *b* as in **b**a**b**y

ch   *ch* as in **ch**icken

d   *d* as in **d**og

ĕ   *e* as in b**e**t

ē   *e* as in compl**e**te, *y* as in hungr**y**

ər   *er* as in butt**er**, *ir* as in b**ir**d, *or* as in doct**or**, *ur* as in **ur**ge

f   *f* as in **f**ast, *ph* as in **ph**one

g   *g* as in **g**ood

h   *h* as in **h**at

ĭ   *i* as in h**i**m

îr   *ier* as in p**ier**, *ear* as in f**ear**

ī   *i* as in **i**ce

j   *j* as in **j**ob

k   *k* as in **k**id, *c* as in **c**ookie

l   *l* as in **l**ie, *le* as in beet**le**

m   *m* as in **m**an

n   *n* as in fu**n**

ŏ   *o* as in m**o**p

ō   *o* as in t**o**e

ô   *o* as in t**o**rn, *a* as in w**a**rm, *aw* as in **aw**kward

oi   *oi* as in n**oi**se, *oy* as in b**oy**

ŏŏ   *oo* as in f**oo**t, *u* as in p**u**t

ow   *ou* as in **out**

p   *p* as in **pin**

r   *r* as in **real**

s   *s* as in **mess**, *c* as in **city**

t   *t* as in **tiny**

th   *th* as in **thin**

th   *th* as in **the**

ŭ   *u* as in **run**, *o* as in **honey**

ū   *u* as in **uniform**

ü   *oo* as in **boot**

yû   *u* as in **cure**, **cute**

v   *v* as in **visit**

w   *w* as in **why**

z   *z* as in **zombie**

zh   *si* as in **vision**, *ge* as in **garage**

Appendix D
Prefixes, Suffixes, and Word Roots

PREFIXES

The following table lists the most common English language prefixes, their meanings, and several examples of words with each prefix. Whenever possible, the examples include both common words that are already part of your everyday vocabulary and words from the lessons in this book.

PREFIX	MEANING	EXAMPLES
a-, an-	not, without	atypical, anarchy, amorphous
ab-, abs-	from, away, off	abnormal, abduct, abscond
ante-	prior to, in front of, before	antedate, antecedent, antebellum
ant-, anti-	opposite, opposing, against	antidote, antagonist, antipathy
bi-	two, twice	bisect, bilateral, bicameral
circum-	around, about, on all sides	circumference, circumnavigate, circumspect
co-, com-, con-	with, together, jointly	community, consensus, cooperate
contra-	against, contrary, contrasting	contradict, contraindication
counter-	contrary, opposite or opposing; complementary	counterclockwise, countermeasure, counterpart
de-	do the opposite or reverse of; remove from, reduce	deactivate, dethrone, detract
dis-	away from, apart, reversal, not	disperse, dismiss, disinterested
duo-	two	duo, duet, duality
ex-	out, out of, away from	expel, exclaim, exorbitant

PREFIX	MEANING	EXAMPLES
in- **(also il-, im-, ir-)**	in, into, within	induct, impart, inculcate
in- **(also il-, im-, ir-)**	not	invariable, incessant, illicit, inept, impervious
inter-	between, among, within	intervene, interact, intermittent
intra-	within, during	intramural, intravenous
intro-	in, into, within	introvert, introduction
mal-	bad, abnormal, evil, wrong	malfunction, malpractice, malign
mis-	bad, wrong, ill; opposite; lack of	misspell, miscreant, misanthrope
mono-	one, single, alone	monologue, monogamy, monocle
multi-	many, multiple	multiple, multimillionaire, multifarious
neo-	new, recent, a new form of	neologism, neonatal, neophyte
non-	not	nonconformist, nonentity, nonchalant
over-	exceeding, surpassing, excessive	overabundance, overstimulate
poly-	many, much	polyester, polytechnic, polyglot
post-	after, subsequent, later (than), behind	postpone, postpartum, postoperative
pre-	before	precaution, precede, presage
pro-	(a) earlier, before, prior to; in front of; (b) for, supporting, in behalf of; (c) forward, projecting	proceed, proclivity, profess
pseudo-	false, fake	pseudonym, pseudoscience
re-	back, again	recall, reconcile, rescind
semi-	half, partly, incomplete	semiannual, semiconscious
sub-	under, beneath, below	subconscious, subdue, subjugate
super-	above, over, exceeding	superhero, superficial, supercilious
trans-	across, beyond, through	transmit, translate, translucent
tri-	three, thrice	triangle, tricycle, triumvirate
un-	not	unable, uninterested, unorthodox
uni-	one	unite, uniform, unilateral

SUFFIXES

The following table lists the most common English language suffixes, their meanings, and several examples of words with each suffix. Whenever possible, the examples include both common words that are already part of your everyday vocabulary and words from the lessons in this book.

NOUN ENDINGS

SUFFIX	MEANING	EXAMPLES
-age	(a) action or process (b) house or place of (c) state, rank	drainage, orphanage, marriage
-al	action or process	rehearsal, disposal, reversal
-an, -ian	of or relating to; a person specializing in	guardian, pediatrician, historian
-ance, -ence	action or process; state of	adolescence, benevolence, renaissance
-ancy, -ency	quality or state	agency, vacancy, latency
-ant, -ent	one that performs, promotes, or causes an action; being in a specified state or condition	disinfectant, dissident, miscreant
-ary	thing belonging to or connected with	adversary, dignitary, library
-cide	killer, killing	suicide, pesticide, homicide
-cy	action or practice; state or quality of	democracy, legitimacy, supremacy
-er, -or	one that is, does, or performs	builder, foreigner, sensor
-ion, -tion	act or process; state or condition	attraction, persecution, denunciation
-ism	act, practice, or process; state or doctrine of	criticism, anachronism, imperialism
-ist	one who (performs, makes, produces, believes, etc.)	anarchist, feminist, imperialist
-ity	quality, state, or degree	clarity, amity, veracity
-ment	action or process; result, object, means, or agent of an action or process	entertainment, embankment, amazement
-ness	state, condition, quality, or degree	happiness, readiness, goodness
-ology	doctrine, theory, or science; oral or written expression	biology, theology, eulogy
-or	condition, activity	candor, valor, succor
-sis	process or action	diagnosis, dialysis, metamorphosis
-ure	act or process; office or function	exposure, legislature, censure
-y	state, condition, quality; activity or place of business	laundry, empathy, anarchy

ADJECTIVE ENDINGS

SUFFIX	MEANING	EXAMPLES
-able, -ible	capable or worthy of; tending or liable to	flammable, culpable, inscrutable
-al, -ial, -ical	having the quality of; of, relating to, or characterized by	educational, peripheral, ephemeral
-an, -ian	one who is or does; related to, characteristic of	human, American, agrarian
-ant, -ent	performing (a specific action) or being (in a specified condition)	important, incessant, preeminent
-ful	full of; having the qualities of; tending or liable to	helpful, peaceful, wistful
-ic	pertaining or relating to; having the quality of	fantastic, chronic, archaic
-ile	tending to or capable of	fragile, futile, servile
-ish	having the quality of	Swedish, bookish, squeamish
-ive	performing or tending toward (an action); having the nature of	sensitive, cooperative, pensive
-less	without, lacking; unable to act or be acted on (in a specified way)	endless, fearless, listless
-ous, -ose	full of, having the qualities of, relating to	adventurous, glorious, egregious
-y	characterized by, full of; tending or inclined to	sleepy, cursory, desultory

VERB ENDINGS

SUFFIX	MEANING	EXAMPLES
-ate	to make, to cause to be or become	violate, tolerate, exacerbate, emanate
-en	to cause to be or have; to come to be or have	quicken, lengthen, frighten
-ify, -fy	to make, form into	beautify, electrify, rectify
-ize	to cause to be or become; to bring about	colonize, plagiarize, synchronize

WORD ROOTS

The following table lists the most common word roots, their meanings, and several examples of words with those roots. Whenever possible, the examples include both common words that are already part of your everyday vocabulary and words from the chapters in this book.

There are more than 150 roots here, but don't be intimidated by the length of this list. Break it down into manageable chunks of 10–20 roots and memorize them section by section. Remember that you use words with these roots every day.

ROOT	MEANING	EXAMPLES
ac, acr	sharp, bitter	acid, acute, acrimonious
act, ag	to do, to drive, to force, to lead	agent, enact, agitate
ad, al	to, toward, near	adjacent, adhere, allure
al, ali, alter	other, another	alternative, alias, alien
am	love	amiable, amity, enamor
amb	to go, to walk	ambulatory, preamble, ambush
amb, amph	both, more than one, around	ambiguous, ambivalent, amphitheater
anim	life, mind, soul, spirit	unanimous, animosity, equanimity
annui, ennui	year	annual, anniversary, perennial
anthro, andr	man, human	anthropology, android, misanthrope
apo	away	apology, apocalypse, apotheosis
apt, ept	skill, fitness, ability	adapt, adept, inept
arch, archi, archy	chief, principal, ruler	hierarchy, monarchy, anarchy
auto	self	automatic, autonomy, automaton
be	to be, to have a certain quality	befriend, bemoan, belittle
bel, bell	war	rebel, belligerent, antebellum
ben, bon	good	benefit, benevolent, bonus
cad, cid	to fall, to happen by chance	accident, coincidence, cascade
cant, cent, chant	to sing	chant, enchant, recant
cap, capit, cipit	head, headlong	capital, principal, capitulate
cap, cip, cept	to take, to get	capture, intercept, emancipate
card, cord, cour	heart	encourage, cardiac, discord
carn	flesh	carnivore, reincarnation, carnage
cast, chast	cut	caste, chastise, castigate
ced, ceed, cess	to go, to yield, to stop	exceed, concede, incessant
centr	center	central, concentric, eccentric
cern, cert, cret, crim, crit	to separate, to judge, to distinguish, to decide	ascertain, critique, discern
chron	time	chronic, chronology, synchronize
cis	to cut	scissors, precise, incisive
cla, clo, clu	shut, close	closet, enclose, preclude
claim, clam	to shout, to cry out	exclaim, proclaim, clamor
cli, clin	to lean toward, bend	decline, recline, proclivity
cour, cur	running, a course	recur, incursion, cursory
crat, cracy	to govern	democracy, autocracy, bureaucracy
cre, cresc, cret	to grow	creation, increase, increment
cred	to believe, to trust	incredible, credit, incredulous
cryp	hidden	crypt, cryptic, cryptography
cub, cumb	to lie down	succumb, incubate, incumbent
culp	blame	culprit, culpable, exculpate

ROOT	MEANING	EXAMPLES
dac, doc	to teach	doctor, indoctrinate, docile
dem	people	democracy, epidemic, pandemic
di, dia	apart, through	dialogue, diatribe, dichotomy
dic, dict, dit	to say, to tell, to use words	predict, dictionary, indict
dign	worth	dignity, indignant, disdain
dog, dox	opinion	dogma, orthodox, paradox
dol	suffer, pain	condolence, indolence, dolorous
don, dot, dow	to give	donate, endow
dub	doubt	dubious, indubitable, dubiety
duc, duct	to lead	conduct, induct, conducive
dur	hard	endure, durable, obdurate
dys	faulty, abnormal	dysfunctional, dystopia, dyslexia
epi	upon	epidemic, epigram, epigraph
equ	equal, even	equation, equanimity, equivocate
err	to wander	err, error, erratic
esce	becoming	adolescent, coalesce, acquiesce
eu	good, well	euphoria, eulogy, euthanasia
fab, fam	speak	fable, famous, affable
fac, fic, fig, fait, feit, fy	to do, to make	fiction, factory, feign
fer	to bring, to carry, to bear	offer, transfer, proliferate
ferv	to boil, to bubble	fervor, fervid, effervescent
fid	faith, trust	confide, fidelity, infidel
fin	end	final, finite, affinity
flag, flam	to burn	flame, flammable, inflammatory
flect, flex	to bend	deflect, reflect, flexible
flu, flux	to flow	fluid, fluctuation, superfluous
fore	before	foresight, forestall, forebear
fort	chance	fortune, fortunate, fortuitous
fra, frac, frag, fring	to break	fracture, fraction, infringe
fus	to pour	confuse, infusion, diffuse
gen	birth, creation, race, kind	generous, genetics, homogenous
gn, gno	to know	ignore, recognize, incognito
grad, gress	to step	progress, aggressive, digress
grat	pleasing	grateful, gratitude, ingratiate
her, hes	to stick	cohere, adherent, inherent
hetero	different, other	heterosexual, heterogeneous, heterodox
(h)om	same	homogeneous, homonym, anomaly
hyper	over, excessive	hyperactive, hyperextend, hyperbole

ROOT	MEANING	EXAMPLES
id	one's own	idiom, idiosyncrasy, ideology
ject	to throw, to throw down	eject, dejected, conjecture
join, junct	to meet, to join	joint, junction, juxtapose
jur	to swear	jury, perjury, abjure
lect, leg	to select, to choose	election, select, eclectic
lev	lift, light, rise	elevator, lever, alleviate
loc, log, loqu	word, speech	dialogue, eloquent, loquacious
luc, lum, lus	light	illustrate, lucid, luminous
lud, lus	to play	illusion, elude, allude
lug, lut, luv	to wash	lavatory, dilute, deluge
mag, maj, max	big	magnify, magnitude, magnanimous
man	hand	manual, manufacture, manifest
min	small	minute, diminish, minutiae
min	to project, to hang over	prominent, imminent, preeminent
mis, mit	to send	transmit, remit, intermittent
mon, monit	to warn	monitor, admonish, remonstrate
morph	shape	amorphous, metamorphosis, anthropomorphic
mort	death	immortal, morbid, moratorium
mut	change	mutate, immutable, permutation
nam, nom, noun, nown, nym	rule, order	economy, taxonomy, autonomy
nat, nas, nai	to be born	native, nascent, renaissance
nec, nic, noc, nox	harm, death	innocent, noxious, innocuous
nom, nym, noun, nown	name	nominate, homonym, nominal
nounc, nunc	to announce	announce, pronounce, denounce
nov, neo, nou	new	novice, novel, neophyte
ob, oc, of, op	toward, to, against, completely, over	object, obstruct, obsequious
omni	all	omnipresent, omnipotent, omniscient
pac, peas	peace	pacify, appease, pacifier
pan	all, everyone	panorama, pandemic, panacea
par	equal	par, disparate, parity
para	next to, beside	parallel, paragon, paradox
pas, pat, path	feeling, suffering, disease	passionate, antipathy, apathetic
pau, po, pov, pu	few, little, poor	poverty, pauper, impoverish
ped	child, education	pediatrician, encyclopedia, pedantic
ped, pod	foot	pedestrian, expedite, impede
pen, pun	to pay, to compensate	penalty, punishment, penance
pend, pens	to hang, to weigh, to pay	depend, compensate, pensive

ROOT	MEANING	EXAMPLES
per	completely, wrong	perplex, permeate, pervade
peri	around	perimeter, peripheral, peripatetic
pet, pit	to go, to seek, to strive	compete, petition, impetuous
phil	love	philosophy, philanthropy, bibliophile
phone	sound	telephone, homophone, cacophony
plac	to please	placid, placebo, complacent
ple	to fill	complete, deplete, plethora
plex, plic, ply	to fold, to twist, to tangle, to bend	complex, comply, implicit
pon, pos, pound	to put, to place	expose, component, juxtapose
port	to carry	import, portable, importune
prehend, prise	to take, to get, to seize	surprise, apprehend, reprisal
pro	much, for, a lot	proliferate, profuse, proselytize
prob	to prove, to test	probe, probation, reprobate
pug	to fight	repugnant, pugnacious, impugn
punc, pung, poign	to point, to prick	point, puncture, punctilious
que, quis	to seek	inquisitive, conquest, query
qui	quiet	quiet, tranquil, acquiesce
rid, ris	to laugh	riddle, ridiculous, derision
rog	to ask	interrogate, surrogate, abrogate
sacr, sanct, secr	sacred	sacred, sacrament, sanction
sal, sil, sault, sult	to leap, to jump	assault, insolent, desultory
sci	to know	conscious, science, omniscient
scribe, scrip	to write	scribble, prescribe, circumscribe
se	apart	separate, segregate, seditious
sec, sequ	to follow	consequence, sequel, obsequious
sed, sess, sid	to sit, to be still, to plan, to plot	subside, assiduous, dissident
sens, sent	to feel, to be aware	sense, sentiment, dissent
sol	to loosen, to free	dissolve, resolution, dissolution
spec, spic, spit	to look, to see	perspective, speculation, circumspect
sta, sti	to stand, to be in place	static, obstinate, steadfast
sua	smooth	suave, persuade, dissuade
tac, tic	to be silent	tacit, reticent, taciturn
tain, ten, tent, tin	to hold	detain, sustain, tenacious
tend, tens, tent, tenu	to stretch, to thin	extend, tension, tenuous
theo	god	atheist, theology, apotheosis
tract	to drag, to pull, to draw	attract, detract, tractable
us, ut	to use	abuse, utility, usurp

ROOT	MEANING	EXAMPLES
ven, vent	to come, to move toward	convene, venture, intervene
ver	truth	verdict, verisimilitude, veritable
vers, vert	to turn	revert, aversion, versatile
vi	life	vivid, vigorous, vicarious
vid, vis	to see	evident, survey, visionary
voc, vok	to call	vocal, advocate, equivocate
vol	to wish	volunteer, volition, benevolence

Notes